Beef
Today!

Company's
Coming
COOKBOOKS

To: Dennis "Joan

I love you both!

Oct 5/97

Beef Today!

Recipes for Today's Lifestyle

Copyright © 1996 by The Recipe Factory Inc.

Second printing October 1996

Canadian Cataloguing in Publication Data

Beef Today! : recipes for today's lifestyle

Includes index.

ISBN 1-896891-00-4

1. Cookery (Beef)

TX749.5.B43B45 1996   641.6'62   C96-900799-X

Every recipe in Beef Today! has been kitchen-tested then approved for publication.
All are true to the Company's Coming tradition of quick and easy recipes using everyday ingredients.

Beef Today! was created thanks to the dedicated efforts of the people and organizations listed on this page.

We extend a special thank you to the Beef Information Centre for permission to use selected recipes and photos and for their support and assistance in this project. Research contributions were also made by the Canadian Cattlemen's Association and Alberta Cattle Commission, Agriculture Canada and Alberta Agriculture, and the National Cattlemen's Beef Association.

Company's Coming Publishing Limited

Chairwoman	Jean Paré
President	Grant Lovig
Production Manager	Kathy Knowles
Production Coordinator	Derrick Sorochan
Production Assistants	Marlene Crosbie, Debbie Dixon

The Recipe Factory Inc.

Managing Editor	Nora Prokop
Research Assistant	Lynda Elsenheimer
Editor/Proofreader	Stephanie With
Test Kitchen Staff	Mary Boratynec, Betty Boychuk
	Ellen Bunjevac, Audrey Thomas
	Pat Yukes
Food Stylist	Stephanie With
Prop Stylist	Gabriele McEleney
Photography	Stephe Tate Photo
Nutrition Analyst	Margaret Ng B.Sc., M.A., R.D.

Design and layout by Boldface Technologies Inc., Edmonton, Alberta, Canada.

Color separations, printing and binding by Friesens, Altona, Manitoba, Canada.

The following businesses generously provided props for use in the photos...

Eaton's
IKEA
The Bay

Chintz & Company
Creations By Design
Enchanted Kitchen
La Cache
Libicz's kitchen essentials
Western Marble Craft (1986) Ltd.

Boston Pizza
Call The Kettle Black

Clayworks Studios
Dufferin Game Room Store
Edmonton Wedding & Party Centre
Le Gnome
Mystique Pottery & Gifts
Off The Wall Gallery
One Island Antique
Stokes
Trail Appliances Ltd.
Tierra Sol Ceramic Tile Ltd.

Published simultaneously in Canada and the United States of America by The Recipe Factory Inc. in conjunction with Company's Coming Publishing Limited
2311 - 96 Street, Edmonton
Alberta, Canada T6N 1G3
Tel: (403) 450-6223 Fax: (403) 450-1857

Printed in Canada

COOKBOOKS

Front cover photo: Herbed Beef Tenderloin, page 107
Contents page photo: Three Pepper Stir-Fry, page 170

Contents

Foreword

BEEF HAS BEEN A STAPLE IN North American diets for well over a century. For a period of time during the mid '70s, beef consumption declined as new products competed for their turn at the dinner table. Today's beef has adapted to our more health-conscious lifestyles. It is leaner, lower in cholesterol and is still one of the best sources of protein and iron. Beef today is available in a wider variety of cuts than ever before, from traditional roasts and steaks to the more modern stir-fry strips, rouladen and pre-seasoned, pre-stuffed roasts or steaks. That's good news for busy, on-the-go individuals and families who demand the convenience of ready-to-cook meats. Beef is back!

Included in this book are both contemporary and traditional long-time favorite recipes. *Hearty Beef Stew, Beef Bourguignonne* and *Porcupine Meatball Stew* are three familiar examples, along with *Spaghetti Meat Sauce, Seasoned Sirloin* and *Classic Meatloaf.* Why do these favorites continue to be a part of today's mealtime? Simply because they are easy to prepare using leaner beef, fresh ingredients and less cooking oil. Each of these recipes maintains a satisfying flavor and pleasing texture while providing a healthier, low-fat alternative.

The goal of our test kitchen staff was twofold: to reduce fat content, and to find simple alternatives to using pre-packaged ingredients, all while maintaining the Company's Coming tradition of creating quick and easy recipes using everyday ingredients.

The first and easiest way to lower fat content without changing the integrity of the recipe was by using leaner beef. Lean ground beef was used in all recipes requiring ground beef, although in many cases extra lean could be considered as a substitute. All cuts of meat were trimmed to ¼ inch (6 mm) or less of fat. Our second step was to use a non-stick skillet or wok when the recipe called for frying or stir-frying. We found that we could eliminate the need for oil entirely in many of the recipes, relying instead upon fat released from the beef during cooking. The third step was to drain off excess fat, if any.

Our second objective, to reduce the number of pre-packaged ingredients, was easier than we anticipated. We were concerned that you might miss the convenience of packaged goods. However, we found that most pre-packaged or prepared items were easily substituted using ingredients already found in your kitchen. Canned tomato sauce for example, or even canned tomatoes mixed with some herbs and spices, make a tasty substitute for ketchup, saving loads of calories in the process. For the more industrious chef, homemade beef stock cooked in batches and frozen in small quantities is a good alternative to canned broth or consommé. Creamed sauces prepared with 1% milk can take the place of canned soups.

We were also careful to watch the amount of beef allocated per serving. The cuts of beef we chose were generally boneless and well-trimmed, resulting in less waste. Today's recommended serving is 3-3½ oz. (85-100 g) of cooked beef per person. Although a healthy, growing 15-year-old might disagree, we felt this was a good average to base our number of servings on. Thus, 1 lb. (454 g) of raw, lean beef yields about 12 oz. (340 g) cooked beef or about 4 servings. The yield will vary slightly depending on the leanness of the beef.

And so we present **Beef Today!**, a complete and carefully compiled guide for using beef in your everyday cooking. Refer to the information on pages 6, 7 and 8 to help you select cuts of beef that will best suit the cooking method you prefer. Can't find the cut suggested in the recipe? Simply look to the *Beef Cuts Substitution Chart* on page 6 to pick a comparable cut that will work just as well. Also included is a helpful chart of *Kitchen Equivalents* on page 186. Make your meal planning easier by browsing through the extensive *Index* at the back of the book, or let it help you out in a pinch when you have a particular cut of beef already defrosted and aren't quite sure what to make.

Flavorful, versatile and healthy, today's beef is featured at its delicious best in over 200 recipes. Whatever you choose, be it appetizer or soup, barbecue or stir fry, for entertaining or everyday cooking, make it **Beef Today!**

Beef is Good for You!

TODAY'S LEANER BEEF continues to be a major dietary source of protein, iron, zinc and the family of B vitamins.

Protein provided by beef is referred to as a 'complete' protein because it is made up of all the essential amino acids that the body must have for good health but cannot make itself. One 3-3½ oz. (85-100 g) serving of cooked lean beef provides almost ⅓ of a man's daily protein needs, and nearly ½ for a woman.

A good store of iron in the body helps keep us alert, energetic and healthy. Red meat, particularly beef, is our best source of iron and is more readily absorbed by the body than iron found in legumes or green vegetables.

Zinc is a component of every living cell in the body. It is essential for growth and reproduction, night vision, digestion and appetite (enhancing our sense of taste and smell). Zinc is critical for maintaining the body's immune system and healing process. Beef's high zinc content is more readily utilized by the body than zinc found in legumes, grains or vegetables.

B vitamins regulate the many chemical reactions in your body necessary to promote growth and maintain health. Some help to release energy, some help to maintain good vision and healthy skin, and others are involved in the manufacture of red blood cells. Vitamin B12 is only found in foods of animal origin such as beef.

Trimming the Fat

The best way to reduce blood levels of cholesterol is to reduce your total daily fat intake from all sources. Much of the saturated fat in beef is in the external layer of fat, which can be trimmed away. Today's lean beef is trimmed to ¼ inch (6 mm) or less. Regular ground beef has a maximum fat content of 30%, lean a maximum of 17% and extra lean no more than 10%.

Another way to 'trim the fat' is during the cooking process. Use a vegetable spray in place of butter, margarine or oil when browning beef or brown in the oven without adding any fat. Use a non-stick skillet or wok with little or no fat. To reduce fat further:

1 Stir-fry in broth instead of oil;

2 Reduce oil to 1 tsp. (5 mL) per ½ cup (125 mL) in marinades, or better yet, eliminate oil altogether;

3 Substitute low-fat or non-fat products for regular dairy products such as sour cream, cream cheese, Cheddar cheese and cottage cheese;

4 Chill soups and stews overnight, then remove solidified fat from the surface before reheating and serving.

Safe Handling and Storage

To handle raw beef safely…

1 Wash your hands before and after handling raw beef;

2 To avoid cross-contamination:

♦ Never let raw beef come in contact with cooked beef or any other edible food item;

♦ Clean working surface and utensils immediately after preparing raw beef;

♦ If wanting to serve the marinade as a sauce, either divide into 2 portions, using one portion for marinating and basting and the other for serving, or bring the marinade to a full rolling boil and boil for 5 minutes after the beef has been removed.

To store beef safely…

1 Refrigerate raw beef at 32-40°F (0-4°C) for up to 4 days; ground beef for up to 2 days;

2 Place wrapped raw beef in a shallow dish in the refrigerator to safeguard against leaking onto other foods;

3 Keep vacuum-packed beef sealed and refrigerated or frozen until ready to use;

4 Cover and refrigerate leftover cooked beef within 1 hour;

5 Store leftover cooked beef wrapped tightly in the refrigerator for up to 7 days or in the freezer for up to 3 months;

6 Cover and refrigerate beef sandwiches for no more than 24 hours and serve chilled to prevent spoilage;

7 Larger pieces of beef (raw or cooked) keep longer chilled or frozen than smaller cuts or cut-up beef;

8 Freeze raw beef in its original packaging for up to 2 weeks. For longer periods (up to 6 months), re-wrap beef in freezer-safe plastic film, heavy-duty aluminum foil or freezer paper. Do not re-freeze raw beef once it has been thawed.

Too Pink or Not Too Pink…

Should contamination occur, it will affect the surface of beef. Once roasts, steaks, cubes or strips have been browned on all sides (or cooked so that the outer surface is completely browned), bacteria has been destroyed. Any red or pink beef inside will be safe to ingest. Ground beef, on the other hand, has been put through a process whereby the original exposed surface has now been ground in, making contamination throughout the beef more likely. That is why ground beef used in any recipe should be cooked until no pink remains and juices are clear.

Choosing Beef
THERE ARE FOUR THINGS TO note when choosing your beef: grading, color, type of cut, and size.

Grading of beef in both Canada and the United States is a means of ensuring beef quality so that you will have maximum eating satisfaction. Grading is about quality and should not be confused with meat inspection. All beef is government-inspected to ensure that it is safe and wholesome. Once this is determined, beef may or may not be graded by qualified graders. The grading systems in each country differs, but both are based on several criteria, the most critical of which is the age of the animal and the amount of marbling in the beef. Marbling is the small, paper-thin veins of fat that criss-cross the beef and add flavor and juiciness.

In Canada you would look for "Canada A, AA, AAA" while in the USA you would look for the comparable grades of "USDA Prime, Choice and Select". These are the top grades and denote the varying levels of marbling. The beef sold by any particular retailer may vary. Check with your local butcher, meat manager or government agricultural department for specific grading information.

There are many natural variations in the color of beef. A very fresh cut piece of beef is blue-red until "bloom" (oxygenation of the blood) occurs, turning the beef a brighter red. Bloom occurs about 30 minutes after exposure and will be maintained for a day or so provided the meat is exposed to air. Retail plastic wrap "breathes", allowing oxygen on the surface of the beef. Patches of graying on the surface are caused by the overlapping of one package, or one item, on the other and cutting off the oxygen. Once the beef is exposed to air the brighter color should return. Discolored beef that has a foul odor should not be used, or at least that portion should be cut off. Government regulations prohibit the use of any additives, preservatives or artificial coloring in beef.

Choosing the right cut of beef for your preferred style of cooking is simple using the information found on pages 7 and 8 of this book.

The size or amount of beef you purchase will depend largely on your personal preferences and budget. How many servings do you need? Do you want to freeze a portion? Is it boneless? How much can you afford to spend? Lean, boneless beef will yield 3-4 servings/pound (6-8 servings/kg). Save shopping and cooking time by purchasing a roast or steak that will yield enough servings for several meals or cook it on the weekend and have leftover beef for those busy weekdays.

To determine your cost per serving, divide the price you pay by the number of servings you will probably get. The more bone and other waste the cut of beef has, the fewer number of servings it will make. Quite often the more expensive boneless cuts are more economical. Also, roasts or steaks can be cut into cubes or strips for use in kabobs, stews or stir-frys to give you a better yield per pound. Extend the yield of ground beef by adding rice, pasta, crackers or bread crumbs.

Beef Cuts Substitution Chart
THIS CHART IS INTENDED AS A GUIDE TO HELP YOU SUBSTITUTE one cut of beef for another in a recipe. For best results, it is recommended you stay within the same tenderness grouping in order to maintain the best cooking method. The *Cooking Methods* information, found on page 8, can help you should you decide to substitute a cut of beef with a different degree of tenderness. Keep in mind, too, that if you use a bone-in roast your cooking times will vary (see *Roasting Guide*, page 8).

	ROASTS		STEAKS		OTHER
Tender (Rib, Loin/Short Loin, Sirloin)	Prime Rib/Rib Sirloin/Top Sirloin	Standing Rib/Rib Tenderloin	Prime Rib/Rib Rib-Eye Sirloin/Top Sirloin Strip Loin	T-Bone Tenderloin Wing	Back Ribs
Medium-Tender (Chuck, Hip/Round)	Arm Pot Shoulder Pot Cross-Rib (all cuts) Rump	Blade (all cuts) Round (all cuts) 7-Bone Pot Sirloin Tip/Tip	Blade Round (all cuts)	Cross-Rib Sirloin Tip/Tip	Ground Beef
Less Tender (Brisket, Shank, Flank, Plate/Short Plate)	Brisket Point	Corned Brisket	Flank	Short Rib	Short Ribs Shank Cross-Cut Stew Beef

Beef Cuts

THE TENDERNESS OF A PARTICULAR CUT OF BEEF DEPENDS ON what part of the animal it comes from. Cuts from active muscle areas – the shoulders, flank and hips (or chuck, hip or round, brisket, plate or short plate and flank) – are naturally less tender and leaner. The meat along the backbone – the ribs and loin or short loin – is the most tender. Specific cuts of beef or names you are familiar with may not appear in this chart. Check with your local butcher for further information.

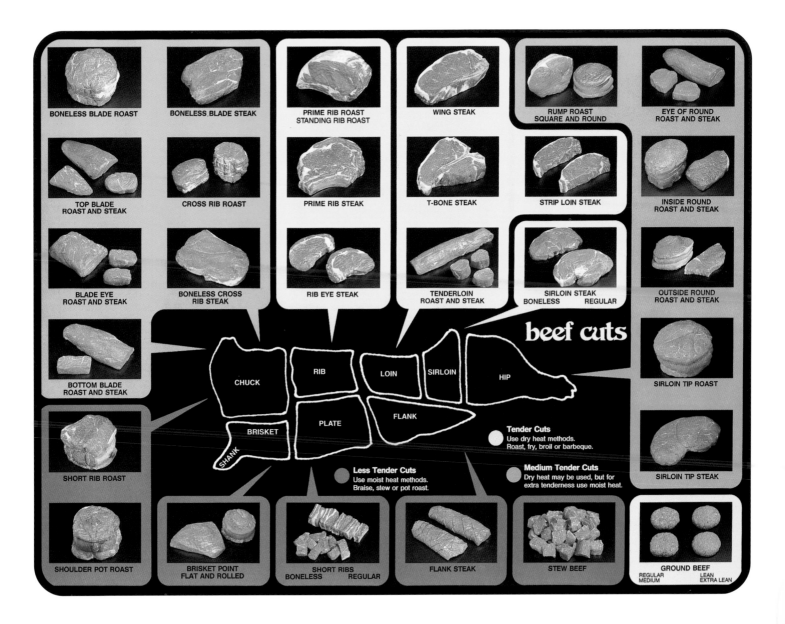

BONELESS BLADE ROAST

BONELESS BLADE STEAK

PRIME RIB ROAST
STANDING RIB ROAST

WING STEAK

RUMP ROAST
SQUARE AND ROUND

EYE OF ROUND
ROAST AND STEAK

TOP BLADE
ROAST AND STEAK

CROSS RIB ROAST

PRIME RIB STEAK

T-BONE STEAK

STRIP LOIN STEAK

INSIDE ROUND
ROAST AND STEAK

BLADE EYE
ROAST AND STEAK

BONELESS CROSS
RIB STEAK

RIB EYE STEAK

TENDERLOIN
ROAST AND STEAK

SIRLOIN STEAK
BONELESS   REGULAR

OUTSIDE ROUND
ROAST AND STEAK

BOTTOM BLADE
ROAST AND STEAK

beef cuts

CHUCK

RIB

LOIN

SIRLOIN

HIP

SIRLOIN TIP ROAST

BRISKET

PLATE

FLANK

SHANK

Tender Cuts
Use dry heat methods.
Roast, fry, broil or barbeque.

SIRLOIN TIP STEAK

SHORT RIB ROAST

Less Tender Cuts
Use moist heat methods.
Braise, stew or pot roast.

Medium Tender Cuts
Dry heat may be used, but for
extra tenderness use moist heat.

SHOULDER POT ROAST

BRISKET POINT
FLAT AND ROLLED

SHORT RIBS
BONELESS   REGULAR

FLANK STEAK

STEW BEEF

GROUND BEEF
REGULAR   LEAN
MEDIUM   EXTRA LEAN

7

Cooking Methods for Beef

THERE ARE TWO main methods for cooking beef – dry heat (roasting, broiling/grilling, barbecuing, frying, stir-frying) and moist heat (braising, stewing, pot roasting). The dry heat method is done without adding liquid; the moist heat method requires enough added liquid to keep the beef moist and help tenderize it during the cooking process.

1 A meat thermometer is recommended to determine the doneness of roasts in both methods. Insert the thermometer into the center of the roast, avoiding any bone or fat.

2 To help retain moisture and improve ease of carving, roasts should be removed from the oven or pot and tented with foil or covered with a lid for 15 minutes before carving. Keep in mind that the temperature of the interior of the roast will rise another 5°F (2°C) during this resting time.

3 Medium-tender and less tender cuts of beef should not be salted before cooking if being browned first. Salt will draw out needed moisture.

Dry Heat Methods

ROASTING: Best for tender roasts. Season as desired. Place, fat side up if any, on a rack in an open roaster. Roast, uncovered, using the *Roasting Guide* below.

BROILING: Best for tender steaks, or medium-tender steaks if marinated beforehand. Place on a broiler rack 4-5 inches (10-12.5 cm) from the heat source. Broil using the *Broiling/Grilling Guide* at lower right.

BARBECUING (GRILLING): Best for tender roasts and steaks, ground beef patties, and for medium-tender roasts and steaks if marinated beforehand. Place 4-5 inches (10-12.5 cm) above the heat source. Barbecue using the *Broiling/Grilling Guide* below.

INDIRECT BARBECUING: Best for medium-tender roasts and steaks if marinated beforehand. Heat the barbecue on one side only. Place beef on unheated side of grill, or move coals from directly under beef. Barbecue using the *Broiling/Grilling Guide* below.

FRYING: Best for tender steaks, or medium-tender steaks if marinated beforehand. Season as desired. Pre-heat a non-stick skillet over medium heat using little or no oil. Place beef in heated skillet and fry on both sides. Refer to the *Broiling/Grilling Guide* below.

STIR-FRYING: Best for tender steak strips, or medium-tender steaks if marinated beforehand. Pre-heat a non-stick skillet or wok over high heat using little or no oil. Brown strips as quickly as possible, turning continuously.

Moist Heat Methods

Marinating or cooking in a mixture containing a food acid such as vinegar, lemon juice or wine will help to break down less tender muscle (connective) tissues. Liquid added can be water, broth, consommé, diluted soup, wine, etc.

BRAISING: Best for medium tender roasts or steaks. For basic roasting, brown roast in a very hot preheated oven, then add 1 cup (250 mL) liquid. Cook, uncovered, using the *Roasting Guide* below. For variations, cook according to the recipe being used. For steaks, brown over medium heat in a non-stick skillet using little or no oil. Pour off any excess drippings. Add liquid and cook according to the recipe being used.

STEWING: Best for less tender roasts or steaks. Beef is cut into cubes or strips and may or may not be coated with flour, depending on the recipe. Brown in either a non-stick skillet using little or no oil over medium heat, or in an ungreased pan in a medium oven. Place in a roaster, large saucepan or Dutch oven. Add liquid and cook, covered, according to the recipe being used.

POT ROASTING: Best for less tender roasts. Roast may or may not be coated with seasoned flour. Brown the roast on all sides, using little or no oil. Cover with liquid and cook, covered, according to the recipe being used.

ROASTING GUIDE

Tenderness	Oven Temperature	Time*		Internal Temperature
Tender	325°F(160°C)	Rare	20min./lb. (45min./kg)	140°F (60°C)
		Medium	25min./lb. (55min./kg)	160°F (70°C)
		Well	30min./lb. (65min./kg)	170°F (75°C)
Medium-Tender	Step 1. 500°F (260°C)	30 minutes total		
	Step 2. (Add liquid)	1¼-1¾ hours total		160°F (70°C)
	275°F (140°C)	(2-5 lb., 1-2.5 kg)		

*Cooking times are based on beef that has been completely thawed. If the roast is frozen, allow about 50% more cooking time. If there is any possibility that the core might still be frozen, insert a small skewer to test. If so, allow extra cooking time and continue to monitor doneness with meat thermometer.

BROILING/GRILLING GUIDE**

Thickness	Minutes per Side		
	Rare	Medium	Well-Done
½-¾ inch (1-2 cm)	2 - 4	5 - 7	7 - 9
1 inch (2.5 cm)	4 - 8	7 - 10	9 - 15
1½ inches (3.8 cm)	7 - 9	8 - 11	10 - 15
2 inches (5 cm)	8 - 14	15 - 20	25 - 30

** Broiling/Grilling times vary depending on distance from heat source, temperature of heat source and the cut of beef. Boneless steaks take less time than bone-in and tender cuts take less time than less tender cuts.

Beef Cooking Tips

APPETIZERS ◆ Use a mini ice cream scoop to measure out uniform-size meatballs. Scoops are available in grocery and retail stores.

◆ To freeze a large quantity of meatballs ahead of time, place drained cooked meatballs in a single layer on a baking sheet. Freeze, uncovered, about 1 hour or until firm. Place in an airtight container. Freeze up to 2 months. Remove as needed.

BARBECUE ◆ For juicier burgers, turn only once and do not flatten while barbecuing.

◆ Use long-handled tongs for turning steaks or roasts; a fork allows flavorful juices to escape. For the same reason, poke the steak with your finger or tongs rather than cutting it with a knife to test for doneness. Rare beef will feel soft, medium will feel springy with some resistance, and well-done will feel hard and unyielding.

◆ Place a drip pan under roasts to prevent flare-ups and grease build-up. Make a drip pan with heavy duty foil or use a shallow foil baking pan.

◆ Marinating roasts and steaks in a plastic bag makes clean-up so easy.

CASSEROLES ◆ Most leftover casseroles can be frozen. Reheat in the oven or in the microwave.

◆ Most casseroles can be made the day before. Quite often the flavor is even better.

◆ Brown beef cubes the day before, store in the refrigerator (or freeze for future use), then complete the recipe the next day. This also applies to pre-browned ground beef mixtures.

◆ Chop extra onions and green peppers. Freeze for future use in casseroles.

◆ When handling jalapeño peppers, wear gloves to prevent burning. Do not get juice on skin or in eyes.

ENTRÉES ◆ Freeze leftover canned broth or consommé in an airtight container for up to 6 months.

◆ When making kabobs, choose vegetables with similar cooking times.

◆ When preparing a dish for the freezer, undercook vegetables and pasta just a little. Additional cooking will occur during the reheating process.

ROASTS ◆ Cube leftover roasts and use in stews and casseroles, or thinly slice for use in sandwiches.

◆ Prepare and cook a roast on the weekend when you have more time. Cook to medium doneness (internal temperature of 160°F, 70°C), then slice, wrap airtight and refrigerate, ready for serving day.

SANDWICHES ◆ To prevent lettuce from wilting when using salad dressing or mayonnaise, put lettuce on one slice of bread and salad dressing on the other. The filling added in between will keep them separate and help maintain crisper lettuce.

SOUPS ◆ Some garnishes work better than others for certain types of soup. Croutons and grated cheese are best in thicker soups while julienned vegetables and pasta work well in clear soups. Snipped fresh herbs can be used in all soups.

◆ Canned stock (broth and consommé) and homemade stock can be used interchangeably but will have different flavors. If desired, simmer canned broth or consommé with finely chopped onion, celery, carrot and parsley for about 30 minutes. Strain before using.

◆ All of the soups in these recipes can be frozen for up to 2 months. Thaw, spoon off any fat and reheat, stirring often.

◆ Cool soups completely before freezing. Fill containers, leaving about ½ inch (12 mm) of head space to allow for expansion.

STEAKS ◆ Cook an extra steak and use the next day, sliced, in a salad or sandwich.

◆ A cast iron skillet works best for searing tender steaks. A small amount of oil should be added to the skillet. Turn only once per side.

◆ Make it easier to separate frozen steaks by placing waxed paper, freezer wrap or foil in between each before freezing.

◆ Larger or thicker cuts of beef will continue to cook after they have been removed from the heat source. If not serving immediately, be careful not to overcook.

STEWS ◆ Brown beef cubes a few at a time. Crowding inside the pan causes beef to steam instead of brown.

◆ To brown beef properly, beef cubes need to stick to the pan slightly. Do not move or stir too much as that will inhibit the caramelizing process.

◆ Day-old stew tends to thicken after absorbing more of the liquid. Add a little hot water when reheating, stirring occasionally.

◆ Make a stew the day before then refrigerate overnight. On serving day, remove the fat from the top of the stew. Heat and thicken as directed in the recipe.

STIR-FRYS ◆ Beef, raw or cooked, is much easier to slice thinly when partially frozen.

◆ Five-spice powder is an excellent blend of seasonings used in Chinese cooking to flavor red meats. It may contain star anise, anise seed, clove, cinnamon, peppercorns, cardamom or orange peel and is available in most spice sections of grocery stores.

◆ Because a wok has sloped sides and is deep it requires less oil than in a regular skillet. If using a regular skillet, more oil may have to be added to keep foods from sticking, or use a skillet with a non-stick coating.

◆ Stir-frying is a very fast cooking method. Have all ingredients measured and prepared before beginning, or prepare them in the morning and store, covered, in the refrigerator.

Accompaniments

Brandy Pepper Sauce, page 15

Roasted Garlic Spread

Use as a dip or as a spread for sandwiches.
Makes 1 cup (250 mL) spread.

1	Large garlic bulb	1
½ cup	Part skim ricotta cheese	125 mL
½ cup	Non-fat sour cream	125 mL
⅛ tsp.	Salt	0.5 mL
Dash	White pepper	Dash

■ Wrap the garlic bulb in foil. Bake in a 375°F (190°C) oven for 1 hour. Remove and cool in the foil until it can be handled. Remove the foil. ■ Cut the root end off exposing the inside cloves. Squeeze the cloves out into a small bowl. Mash with a fork. Add the cheese, sour cream, salt and pepper. Mix well. Cover and chill.

1 tbsp. (15 mL) spread… Energy 13cal/53kJ;
Fat 0.6g; Protein 1g; Carbohydrate 1g

Roasted Peppers

Whole green, orange, red or yellow peppers.

■ Place the desired color of pepper on a rack under the broiler, over high heat on the barbecue or, using tongs, directly on a burner (gas is best) on high. Blacken the pepper on all sides and ends. Watch carefully. ■ When mostly blackened, place the pepper in a paper bag and close, or place in a bowl and cover with plastic wrap. ■ When the pepper has cooled enough to handle, remove and discard the skin. Remove the seeds and white ribs and cut according to the directions in the recipe.

One pepper… Energy 20 cal/84kJ;
Fat 0.1g; Protein 1g; Carbohydrate 5g

Creamy Mushroom Pepper Sauce

Spoon 2 tbsp. (30 mL) sauce over a broiled or barbecued steak. Makes 1⅛ cups (280 mL) sauce.

2 tbsp.	Hard margarine	30 mL
3 oz.	Large portobello mushrooms, chopped	56 mL
1 tsp.	Freshly ground pepper	5 mL
2 tsp.	All-purpose flour	10 mL
¾ cup	Skim evaporated milk	175 mL

■ Melt the margarine in a non-stick skillet. Sauté the mushrooms and pepper until the mushrooms are soft. Stir in the flour. Add the evaporated milk and simmer, uncovered, for 5 minutes.

2 tbsp. (30 mL) sauce… Energy 42cal/176kJ;
Fat 2.6g; Protein 2g; Carbohydrate 3g

Béarnaise Sauce

Sides of saucepan should be touchable at all times. Pour 2 tbsp. (30 mL) sauce over each steak. Makes ¾ cup (175 mL) sauce.

1 tbsp.	Minced shallots	15 mL
1 tsp.	Dried tarragon, crumbled	5 mL
⅛ tsp.	White pepper	0.5 mL
½ cup	Dry white wine	125 mL
1 tbsp.	White wine vinegar	15 mL
2	Egg yolks (large)	2
¼ cup	Hard margarine, melted	60 mL
Dash	Cayenne pepper	Dash
1 tsp.	Finely chopped fresh parsley	5 mL

■ Combine the shallots, tarragon, pepper, wine and vinegar in a small saucepan. Bring to a boil. Reduce the heat and simmer, uncovered, for 8 to 10 minutes. Liquid should be reduced to ⅓ cup (75 mL). Strain into a small cup, discarding the shallots. ■ Whisk the egg yolks lightly in a double boiler. Add 1 tbsp. (15 mL) of the melted margarine. Whisk together. Place over barely simmering water. Whisk in the strained liquid and remaining margarine. Continue whisking until fluffy and thickened. ■ Remove from the heat. Stir in the cayenne pepper and the parsley.

2 tbsp. (30 mL) sauce… Energy 49cal/204kJ; Fat 4.3g; Protein 1g; Carbohydrate 1g

Mustard Cream Sauce

Drizzle 2 tbsp. (30 mL) over a seasoned broiled or barbecued steak. Makes 3/4 cup (175 mL) sauce.

2 tsp.	Olive oil	10 mL
½ cup	Finely minced onion	125 mL
½ tsp.	All-purpose flour	2 mL
½ cup	Skim evaporated milk	125 mL
2 tsp.	Dijon mustard	10 mL
¼ tsp.	Salt	1 mL
½ tsp.	Freshly ground pepper	2 mL

■ Heat the oil in a non-stick skillet. Sauté the onion until soft. Sprinkle the flour over the onion and mix well. Whisk in the milk, mustard, salt and pepper. Bring to a boil. Reduce the heat and simmer until thickened.

2 tbsp. (30 mL) sauce… Energy 40cal/170kJ;
Fat 1.8g; Protein 2g; Carbohydrate 4g

Aïoli Sauce

A garlic mayonnaise from Provence, France. Serve with warm or cold Spanish Sirloin, page 41. Makes 1 cup (250 mL) sauce.

3	Garlic cloves, chopped	3
¼ tsp.	Salt	1 mL
1 tbsp.	Lemon juice	15 mL
1	Large egg	1
1 cup	Olive oil	250 mL

■ Combine the garlic, salt, lemon juice and egg in a blender or food processor. Process until creamy. With the machine running, slowly pour the oil through the opening or feed tube. Continue processing until thick. Chill until serving time.

1 tbsp. (15 mL) sauce… Energy 132cal/562kJ;
Fat 14.6g; Protein trace; Carbohydrate trace

Fresh Tomato Salsa

Serve with, or spoon over, Pesto Meatloaf Roll, page 83. Makes 2 cups (500 mL) salsa.

5	Plum tomatoes, seeded and finely chopped	5
2 tbsp.	Olive oil	30 mL
1 tbsp.	Chopped fresh sweet basil	15 mL
1 tbsp.	Chopped fresh parsley	15 mL
1	Garlic clove, minced	1
1 tsp.	Salt	5 mL

■ Combine all the ingredients in a medium bowl. Cover and marinate in the refrigerator for 2 hours.

2 tbsp. (30 mL) salsa… Energy 24cal/99kJ;
Fat 1.8g; Protein trace; Carbohydrate 2g

Stilton Port Sauce

Drizzle 1 tbsp. (15 mL) sauce over a tenderloin steak. Makes ¾ cup (175 mL) sauce.

2 tsp.	Olive oil	10 mL
¼ cup	Finely minced onion	60 mL
1 tsp.	All-purpose flour	5 mL
2 tbsp.	Port wine	30 mL
½ cup	Skim evaporated milk	125 mL
1 tsp.	Worcestershire sauce	5 mL
¼ cup	Crumbled Stilton cheese	60 mL

■ Heat the oil in a small non-stick skillet. Add the onion and sauté for about 2 minutes until soft and golden. Sprinkle with the flour. Mix in well. Whisk in the wine and milk until slightly thickened. Add the Worcestershire sauce and cheese. Heat gently until the cheese is melted.

1 tbsp. (15 mL) sauce… Energy 34cal/143kJ;
Fat 1.7g; Protein 2g; Carbohydrate 2g

Black Bean Salsa

Make a day ahead to allow flavors to blend.
Use in Barbecued Fajitas, page 39. Makes
2 cups (500 mL) salsa.

14 oz.	Canned black beans, with liquid	398 mL
¼ tsp.	Cayenne pepper	1 mL
¼ tsp.	Salt	1 mL
1	Garlic clove, minced	1
1 tsp.	Lime juice	5 mL
½ tsp.	Chili powder	2 mL
½ cup	Finely chopped red onion	125 mL
1	Red Roasted Pepper, page 11, peeled and cut into slivers	1
1 tbsp.	Finely chopped fresh cilantro	15 mL
1	Medium tomato, seeded and diced	1
10	Pitted ripe olives, sliced	10

■ Combine the first 6 ingredients in a saucepan
and simmer for 15 minutes or until some of the
liquid is evaporated and the beans are soft. Stir
often to prevent scorching. Remove from the
heat and add the remaining 5 ingredients. Stir
well and refrigerate.

2 tbsp. (30 mL) salsa… Energy 33cal/140kJ;
Fat trace; Protein 2g; Carbohydrate 6g

Pineapple Salsa

Serve with Holiday Steak, page 41.
Makes 1⅛ cups (280 mL) salsa.

8 oz.	Canned pineapple tidbits, drained	227 mL
½ cup	Chopped red onion	125 mL
2 tbsp.	Chopped fresh cilantro or parsley	30 mL
1 tbsp.	Lime juice	15 mL
½ tsp.	Cayenne pepper	2 mL

■ Combine all the ingredients in a small bowl.
Cover and refrigerate for at least 1 hour to cool
and blend the flavors.

2 tbsp. (30 mL) salsa… Energy 13cal/54kJ;
Fat trace; Protein trace; Carbohydrate 3g

Salsa Romescu

Try this sauce over noodles and serve with steak.
Makes 1 cup (250 mL) salsa.

¼ cup	Slivered almonds	60 mL
1	Garlic clove, chopped	1
¼ tsp.	Cayenne pepper	1 mL
½ tsp.	Salt	2 mL
1	Small tomato, peeled, seeded and chopped	1
¼ cup	Red wine vinegar	60 mL
1 tbsp.	Chopped fresh parsley	15 mL
¾ cup	Olive oil	175 mL

■ Combine the almonds, garlic, cayenne pepper, salt, tomato, vinegar and parsley in a blender or food processor. Purée. ■ With the machine still running, slowly pour the oil through the opening or feed tube. Process until thick. Chill until serving time.

2 tbsp. (30 mL) salsa… Energy 205cal/857kJ;
Fat 22.1g; Protein 1g; Carbohydrate 2g

Herbed Butter

The color of the fresh basil looks best. Serve on hot steak.
Makes 12 pats of flavored butter, ¼ inch (6 mm) thick.

½ cup	Butter, softened	125 mL
1	Garlic clove, crushed	1
2 tbsp.	Finely minced fresh parsley	30 mL
1½ tsp.	Finely minced fresh sweet basil (or ½ tsp., 2 mL dried)	7 mL
½ tsp.	Dried thyme, crumbled	2 mL

■ Combine the butter with the garlic and herbs. Mix well. Refrigerate to firm slightly. Place on waxed paper and form into a 1 inch (2.5 cm) roll. Roll up in the waxed paper and chill well before cutting into ¼ inch (6 mm) pats.

One pat… Energy 73cal/303kJ; Fat 8.1g; Protein trace; Carbohydrate trace

Herb Cheese Spread

Spread this on baguettes or fresh bread slices and serve with steak. Makes 6 small balls.

1 tbsp.	Chopped fresh chives	15 mL
1 tsp.	Finely chopped fresh sweet basil	5 mL
¼ tsp.	Crushed green peppercorns	1 mL
4 oz.	Light cream cheese	125 g

■ Combine the fresh herbs and peppercorns in a shallow bowl. Shape the cream cheese into 6 balls and roll in the herb mixture. Cover and refrigerate. Remove from the refrigerator 20 to 30 minutes before serving.

One ball… Energy 48cal/199kJ; Fat 1.2g; Protein 2g; Carbohydrate 1g

Brandy Pepper Sauce

Drizzle 2 tsp. (10 mL) over individual steaks. Makes ½ cup (125 mL) sauce.

¼ cup	Unsalted butter	60 mL
1 tsp.	Olive oil	5 mL
1 tbsp.	Coarsely ground mixed peppercorns	15 mL
1 tbsp.	Finely chopped shallots	15 mL
¼ cup	Brandy	60 mL
¾ cup	Condensed beef broth	175 mL
¼ cup	Whipping cream	60 mL

■ Melt the butter and oil in a small non-stick skillet. Stir in the peppercorns and shallots. Sauté until the shallots are soft. ■ Add the brandy and beef broth. Boil, stirring occasionally, until reduced by ½. Stir in the whipping cream. Boil again for 2 minutes.

2 tsp. (10 mL) sauce… Energy 68cal/285kJ;
Fat 5.7g; Protein 1g; Carbohydrate 1g

CHAPTER 2

Appetizers

Hot Cheese Rounds, page 27

Beefy Pepper Dim Sum

Assemble in the morning. Cover and refrigerate.
Bake just before serving. Makes 24 appetizers.

1	Large green pepper	1
1	Large red pepper	1
1	Large yellow pepper	1
½ lb.	Lean ground beef	225 g
1	Garlic clove, minced	1
½ tsp.	Salt	2 mL
¼ cup	Chopped green onion	60 mL
¼ cup	Finely diced water chestnuts	60 mL
1½ tbsp.	Black bean sauce or soy sauce	25 mL
1	Large egg, fork-beaten	1
1 tbsp.	All-purpose flour	15 mL
1 tbsp.	Toasted sesame seeds	15 mL

■ Cut the peppers in half crosswise. Remove the seeds and white ribs. Cut each half into 4 pieces to make a total of 24. ■ Scramble-fry the beef with the garlic and salt in a non-stick skillet for 4 minutes or until the beef is no longer pink but is still moist. Remove from the heat. ■ Add the onion, water chestnuts, black bean sauce, egg and flour. Mix well. ■ Arrange the pepper pieces inside up on a lightly sprayed baking sheet. Spoon the beef mixture into the pepper pieces. Sprinkle with the toasted sesame seeds. ■ Bake in a 350°F (175°) oven for 10 to 15 minutes.

One appetizer... Energy 26cal/111kJ;
Fat 1.3g; Protein 2g; Carbohydrate 1g

Beef Saté with Peanut Sauce

Soak 36, 4 inch (10 cm) long bamboo skewers in water for 10 minutes while preparing the kabobs. Makes 36 appetizer kabobs.

MARINADE

½ tsp.	Chili powder	2 mL
1 tsp.	Ground cumin	5 mL
1 tsp.	Granulated sugar	5 mL
2 tbsp.	Soy sauce	30 mL
1	Small onion, finely chopped	1
1 tbsp.	Lemon juice	15 mL
1 lb.	Top round steak, cut into ½ inch (12 mm) cubes	454 g

PEANUT SAUCE

1 tsp.	Vegetable oil	5 mL
¼ cup	Finely chopped onion	60 mL
1 tbsp.	Brown sugar	15 mL
2 tbsp.	Lime juice	30 mL
⅓ cup	Crunchy peanut butter	75 mL
⅔ cup	Skim evaporated milk	150 mL
½ tsp.	Chili powder	2 mL

■ Combine the 6 marinade ingredients and pour over the beef cubes in a large bowl. Stir to coat. Cover. Marinate in the refrigerator for 2 hours or longer, stirring several times. Remove the cubes and discard the marinade. ■ Place 3 cubes of beef on each presoaked skewer. Broil the kabobs for 1 minute per side or to desired doneness. ■ Heat the oil in a small saucepan and sauté the onion for 3 to 4 minutes or until soft. Whisk in the brown sugar, lime juice, peanut butter and evaporated milk. Simmer for 2 minutes. Stir in the chili powder and simmer for 1 minute. ■ Serve hot with the kabobs.

One kabob… Energy 35cal/147kJ;
Fat 1.6g; Protein 3g; Carbohydrate 2g

Oriental Mini Beef Skewers

Soak 48, 4 inch (10 cm) long bamboo skewers in water for 10 minutes just before threading on the beef. Makes 48 appetizer kabobs.

1 lb.	Round or flank steak	454 g
MARINADE		
1 tbsp.	Vegetable oil	15 mL
1 tbsp.	Liquid honey	15 mL
¼ cup	Sherry	60 mL
¼ cup	Soy sauce	60 mL
1	Garlic clove, minced	1
1 tsp.	Freshly grated gingerroot	5 mL
1	Green onion, chopped	1
2 tsp.	Sesame seeds	10 mL

■ Slice the beef diagonally across the grain into ⅛ inch (3 mm) thick strips. ■ Thoroughly mix together the 8 marinade ingredients. Add the beef strips and stir to coat. Cover and marinate in the refrigerator 4 hours or overnight, stirring several times. ■ Remove the beef and discard the marinade. Thread, accordion-style, onto the presoaked bamboo skewers. ■ Broil for 2 minutes per side or to desired doneness. ■ Variation: To serve as a main course, thread the beef strips, flattened accordion-style, on 8 inch (20 cm) presoaked bamboo skewers. These will take less time to cook. Broil for 2 minutes on the first side and 1 minute on the second side.

One kabob... Energy 12cal/50kJ;
Fat 0.4g; Protein 2g; Carbohydrate 0.2g

Pineapple Beef Skewers

Soak 24, 4 inch (10 cm) bamboo skewers for 10 minutes in water. Makes 24 kabob appetizers.

¾ lb.	Sirloin tip steak, ½ inch (12 mm) thick	340 g
14 oz.	Canned pineapple chunks, juice reserved	398 mL
24	Maraschino cherries, syrup reserved	24

SAUCE

¾ cup	Reserved pineapple juice	175 mL
¼ cup	Reserved maraschino cherry syrup	60 mL
2	Garlic cloves, crushed	2
1 tbsp.	Minced crystallized ginger	15 mL
3 tbsp.	Liquid honey	50 mL
¼ cup	Soy sauce	60 mL
1 tbsp.	Cornstarch	15 mL

■ Cut the steak into 1 x 1 inch (2.5 x 2.5 cm) pieces. On each skewer, alternate 1 piece of pineapple, 1 piece of beef, 1 cherry, another piece of beef and ending with another piece of pineapple. ■ Combine the 7 sauce ingredients in a small saucepan. Heat until the mixture boils and thickens, stirring constantly. Cool slightly. Poor into a tall narrow container or glass. Dip each skewer into the sauce, letting excess drip off. Lay on a rack in a broiler pan. Broil for 4 minutes per side. Brush with more sauce after turning. ■ Reheat the sauce to boiling and serve hot as a dip for the skewers.

One kabob… Energy 40cal/170kJ;
Fat 0.5g; Protein 3g; Carbohydrate 6g

Beef-Stuffed Mushrooms

Make and freeze the filling ahead. Makes 16 appetizers.

16	Medium fresh mushrooms	16
¼ lb.	Lean ground beef	113 g
2 tbsp.	Finely chopped pine nuts	30 mL
¼ cup	Finely chopped shallots	60 mL
¼ cup	Fresh bread crumbs	60 mL
1	Large egg, fork-beaten	1
3 tbsp.	Chopped sun-dried tomatoes, softened in boiling water 5 minutes before chopping	50 mL
2 tbsp.	Chopped fresh sweet basil	30 mL
¼ tsp.	Salt	1 mL
¼ tsp.	Lemon pepper	1 mL

■ Clean the mushrooms. Remove and discard the stems. ■ Scramble-fry the beef, pine nuts and shallots in a small non-stick skillet until the beef is browned and the shallots are soft. Remove from the heat. Add the bread crumbs, egg, sun-dried tomatoes, basil, salt and lemon pepper. Mix well. ■ Stuff the mushrooms, mounding the filling slightly. Place on an ungreased baking sheet. ■ Bake in a 400°F (205°C) oven for 10 minutes.

One stuffed mushroom… Energy 30cal/124kJ; Fat 1.6g; Protein 2g; Carbohydrate 2g

Roasted Pepper and Beef Triangles

Make, bake and freeze ahead. Reheat in the oven not in the microwave. Makes 84 fancy appetizers.

2 tbsp.	Hard margarine	30 mL
3 cups	Thinly sliced and quartered onion	750 mL
2 tsp.	Brown sugar	10 mL
1 tbsp.	Hard margarine	15 mL
8 oz.	Tenderloin steak, ¾-1 inch (2-2.5 cm) thick, cut into ⅛ x 1 inch (0.3 x 2.5 cm) strips	225 g
1	Garlic clove, minced	1
2 tbsp.	All-purpose flour	30 mL
½ tsp.	Salt	2 mL
¼ tsp.	Freshly ground pepper	1 mL
¾ cup	Condensed beef broth	175 mL
1 tbsp.	Chopped fresh sweet basil	15 mL
⅓ cup	Freshly grated Parmesan cheese	75 mL
8 oz.	Part skim ricotta cheese	250 g
1	Red Roasted Pepper, page 11, peeled and cut in slivers about 1 inch (2.5 cm) long	1
21	Phyllo pastry sheets	21

■ Melt the first amount of margarine in a non-stick skillet. Sauté the onion for 10 minutes, stirring constantly. Reduce the heat and cook for 10 to 20 minutes, stirring frequently, until the onion is browned and caramelized (not burned). Stir in the brown sugar and remove the mixture to a small bowl. ■ Melt the second amount of margarine in the same skillet and sauté the beef strips and garlic for 5 minutes. Stir in the flour, salt and pepper. Add the beef broth, stirring until the mixture bubbles and thickens. Mix in the carmelized onion. Remove from the heat and cool while preparing the pepper mixture. ■ Combine the basil and cheeses with the red pepper and add to the beef mixture. ■ Lay 1 sheet of phyllo pastry on a non-floured working surface. Cover the remainder with a damp tea towel. Lightly spray the pastry sheet. Cut the sheet crosswise into 4 equal strips. Fold each strip in half lengthwise. ■ Place 1 rounded tsp. (5 mL) of filling at one end. Fold 1 corner over to form a triangle. Continue folding over triangles to the end of the strip. Be sure corners of triangle overlap to tightly enclose filling. Spray the top of the final triangle and place other side on a lightly sprayed baking sheet. Repeat with remaining sheets of phyllo. ■ Bake in a 400°F (205°C) oven for about 12 minutes until golden brown.

One triangle… Energy 28cal/117kJ; Fat 1.7g; Protein 1g; Carbohydrate 2g

Beef in a Bread Cup

Best if made fresh. If made ahead, reheat in the oven not in the microwave.
Makes 84 appetizers.

21	Bread slices, crusts removed	21

MEATBALLS

1 lb.	Lean ground beef	454 g
1	Large egg	1
2 tbsp.	Finely chopped onion	30 mL
¾ cup	1% milk	175 mL
1 tsp.	Seasoned salt	5 mL
¼ tsp.	Pepper	1 mL
1 tbsp.	Dijon mustard	15 mL
1 tbsp.	Tomato paste	15 mL
1	Small garlic clove, minced	1
1 cup	Dry bread crumbs	250 mL

GARNISH

Hot pepper jelly
Process cheese slices
Sliced green onion
Prepared mustard

■ Cut each bread slice into 4 quarters and gently push each piece into minimuffin pan cups. ■ Combine the next 10 meatball ingredients in a medium bowl. Mix well. Using 1 rounded tsp. (5 mL) of the mixture, form into balls. Place 1 ball in each bread cup. ■ Bake in a 350°F (175°C) oven for 10 to 15 minutes. Remove. ■ Garnish as desired. If using cheese, return to the oven for 6 minutes.

One appetizer… Energy 34cal/141kJ;
Fat 1.2g; Protein 2g; Carbohydrate 4g

Spanish Meatballs

Serve in a chafing dish or heat-proof bowl with cocktail picks. Makes 36 appetizer meatballs.

MEATBALLS

1 lb.	Lean ground beef	454 g
1 cup	Fresh whole wheat bread crumbs	250 mL
2 tbsp.	1% milk	30 mL
1	Large egg, fork-beaten	1
1	Garlic clove, minced	1
¼ tsp.	Salt	1 mL
¼ tsp.	Pepper	1 mL

SPANISH SAUCE

1	Medium onion, finely chopped	1
2	Garlic cloves, minced	2
1 tbsp.	Olive oil	15 mL
½ tsp.	Beef bouillon powder	2 mL
½ cup	Boiling water	125 mL
1 tbsp.	Tomato paste	15 mL
½ cup	White wine	125 mL
2 tsp.	Cornstarch	10 mL
¼ tsp.	Pepper	1 mL
⅛ tsp.	Ground cloves	0.5 mL
1 tsp.	Brown sugar	5 mL

■ Combine the 7 meatball ingredients in a large bowl and mix well. Roll into 1 inch (2.5 cm) balls and place on an ungreased baking sheet. ■ Bake in a 350°F (175°C) oven for 10 minutes. Drain. ■ Sauté the onion and garlic in the olive oil in a medium saucepan for 2 to 3 minutes or until soft. Dissolve the bouillon powder in the boiling water in a small cup. Add to the onion mixture. Stir in the tomato paste. Mix the wine and cornstarch in a small cup until smooth and stir into the tomato paste mixture. Bring to a boil and stir until thickened and clear. Add the pepper, cloves and brown sugar. ■ Add the meatballs and heat gently for 25 to 30 minutes.

One meatball… Energy 34cal/140kJ; Fat 1.6g; Protein 3g; Carbohydrate 1g

Maple-Glazed Meatballs

Serve warm with cocktail picks. Makes 96 meatballs plus 1¼ cups (300 mL) sauce.

MEATBALLS

1½ lbs.	Lean ground beef	680 g
2 tbsp.	Prepared horseradish	30 mL
1¼ cups	Dry bread crumbs	300 mL
2	Large eggs, fork-beaten	2
½ cup	Skim evaporated milk	125 mL

SAUCE

½ cup	Chili sauce	125 mL
½ cup	Corn or cane syrup	125 mL
2 tbsp.	Soy sauce	30 mL
½ tsp.	Dry mustard powder	2 mL
½ tsp.	Ground allspice	2 mL
2 tsp.	Cornstarch	10 mL
1½ tsp.	Maple flavoring	7 mL

■ Combine the 5 meatball ingredients in a medium bowl. Mix well and form into ¾ inch (2 cm) balls. Place on an ungreased baking sheet.

■ Bake in a 450°F (230°C) oven for 10 minutes.

■ Combine the 7 sauce ingredients in a medium saucepan and heat to boiling, stirring frequently. Add the meatballs and stir to heat through.

1 meatball plus 1 tsp. (5mL) sauce... Energy 25cal/106kJ; Fat 0.7g; Protein 2g; Carbohydrate 3g

Apricot-Glazed Meatballs

Serve these with cocktail picks. Keep warm.
Makes 30 meatballs.

MEATBALLS

1 lb.	Lean ground beef	454 g
⅓ cup	Dry bread crumbs	75 mL
¼ cup	Finely chopped dried apricots	60 mL
1 tsp.	Soy sauce	5 mL
½ tsp.	Chinese five-spice powder	2 mL
1	Small garlic clove, minced	1

APRICOT GLAZE

½ cup	Apricot jam or preserves	125 mL
1 tsp.	Soy sauce	5 mL
2 tsp.	Brown sugar	10 mL
2 tsp.	White vinegar	10 mL
¼ tsp.	Chinese five-spice powder	1 mL
1 tsp.	Cornstarch	5 mL

■ Combine the 6 meatball ingredients in a medium bowl. Mix well. Shape into 30, 1 inch (2.5 cm) balls. Place on an ungreased baking sheet. ■ Bake, uncovered, in a 350°F (175°C) oven for 15 to 20 minutes or until no longer pink. Drain. ■ Mix the first 5 glaze ingredients together in a small saucepan. Heat, stirring occasionally, until boiling. Mix the cornstarch with 1 tbsp. (15 mL) cold water. Stir into the glaze. Continue stirring until thickened. ■ Serve over or beside the meatballs.

One meatball… Energy 37cal/154kJ;
Fat 1.3g; Protein 3g; Carbohydrate 3g

Hot Cheese Rounds

Make the day before or freeze well in advance. No need for re-heating – just bring to room temperature. Makes 36 appetizers.

¾ lb.	Lean ground beef	340 g
½ tsp.	Salt	2 mL
¼ tsp.	Cayenne pepper	1 mL
1½ cups	All-purpose flour	375 mL
1 tbsp.	Baking powder	15 mL
3 tbsp.	Hard margarine	50 mL
1 cup	Grated sharp Cheddar cheese	250 mL
¼ cup	Finely chopped green onion	60 mL
1 tsp.	Worcestershire sauce	5 mL
1 tsp.	Beef bouillon powder	5 mL
⅓ cup	Boiling water	75 mL
	Paprika	

■ Scramble-fry the beef in a non-stick skillet with the salt and cayenne pepper. Drain well. Cool slightly. ■ Combine the flour and baking powder in a large bowl. Cut in the margarine until the mixture is crumbly. Stir in the grated cheese, green onion and slightly cooled beef. ■ Combine the Worcestershire sauce, bouillon powder and water in a small cup. Add to the beef mixture, stirring with a fork until well mixed. ■ Form into 36, 1 inch (2.5 cm) balls and place on a lightly sprayed baking sheet. Press the balls down with a fork and sprinkle with paprika. ■ Bake in a 400°F (205°C) oven for 12 minutes or until the bottoms are slightly browned. ■ Remove from the baking sheet and allow to cool to room temperature before serving.

One appetizer… Energy 58cal/241kJ; Fat 2.9g; Protein 3g; Carbohydrates 4g

Mexican Snackies

Cut into 1½ x 2 inch (3.8 x 5 cm) pieces to serve. Makes 40 appetizers.

2 cups	Biscuit mix	500 mL
¼ cup	Chopped fresh cilantro (coriander)	60 mL
½ cup	Water	125 mL
½ lb.	Lean ground beef	225 g
14 oz.	Canned refried beans with green chilies	398 mL
1 cup	Non-fat sour cream	250 mL
2 tbsp.	Taco seasoning mix (35 g pkg.)	30 mL
1½ cups	Grated medium Cheddar cheese	375 mL
½ cup	Finely chopped green onion	125 mL
¼ cup	Finely chopped green pepper	60 mL
¼ cup	Finely chopped red pepper	60 mL
1 cup	Finely diced and seeded tomatoes	250 mL
¼ cup	Finely chopped pitted ripe olives	60 mL

■ Combine the biscuit mix with the cilantro. Add the water and stir to make a soft dough. Knead about 10 times on a surface lightly coated with biscuit mix. Press into an ungreased 15 x 10 x 1 inch (38 x 25 x 2.5 cm) jelly roll pan. (The dough will be very thin). ■ Bake in a 400°F (205°C) oven for 10 minutes or until golden and firm. Cool. ■ Scramble-fry the beef. Drain. Remove from the heat and stir in the refried beans. Cool slightly before spreading over the crust. ■ Combine the sour cream and seasoning mix. Spread over the beef and beans. Sprinkle with the cheese. ■ Combine the remaining 5 ingredients. Sprinkle the vegetable mixture over the cheese. Pack down slightly with your hand. Chill for 1 hour.

One appetizer… Energy 79cal/330kJ;
Fat 3.3g; Protein 4g; Carbohydrate 9g

Refried Bean Dip

Serve this warm with tortilla chips. Makes 4 cups (1L) dip.

14 oz.	Canned refried beans	398 mL
1 cup	Salsa (mild, medium or hot)	250 mL
1 lb.	Lean ground beef	454 g
	Salt, to taste	
1 cup	Grated medium Cheddar cheese	250 mL
1 cup	Non-fat sour cream	250 mL
2 tbsp.	Finely chopped green onion	30 mL
1 cup	Shredded iceberg lettuce	250 mL
1	Medium tomato, seeded and chopped	1

■ Combine the beans with 2 tsp. (10 mL) of the salsa. Spread evenly in an ungreased 10 inch (25 cm) pie plate. ■ Scramble-fry the beef in a non-stick skillet until browned. Drain. Add ½ cup (125 mL) of the salsa and the salt and cook for 5 minutes. Spread the beef evenly over the beans. Sprinkle with the cheese. ■ Bake in a 350°F (175°C) oven for 15 minutes until the cheese is melted and the beans are hot. Remove from the oven and let cool for 10 minutes.
■ Spread with the remaining salsa. Mix the sour cream and onion and spread over salsa. Sprinkle with the lettuce and tomato.

2 tbsp. (30mL) dip… Energy 56cal/234kJ; Fat 2.6g; Protein 5g; Carbohydrate 4g

Beef Sprout Rolls

Assemble in the morning and keep well-covered with a damp towel until just before baking. Makes 32 rolls.

1 tbsp.	Vegetable oil	15 mL
½ cup	Finely chopped onion	125 mL
½ cup	Finely chopped celery	125 mL
1½ cups	Coarsely chopped fresh bean sprouts	375 mL
½ cup	Grated carrot	125 mL
½ lb.	Lean ground beef	225 g
1	Garlic clove, minced	1
2 tbsp.	Black bean sauce	30 mL
2	Large eggs, fork-beaten	2
⅛ tsp.	Salt	0.5 mL
⅛ tsp.	Freshly ground pepper	0.5 mL
8	Phyllo pastry sheets	8
2 tbsp.	Hard margarine, melted	30 mL
1 tbsp.	Toasted sesame seeds	15 mL

■ Heat the oil in a non-stick skillet until hot. Add the onion, celery, bean sprouts and carrot. Stir-fry for 5 minutes. Empty into a medium bowl. ■ Scramble-fry the beef and garlic in the same skillet until browned. Drain. ■ Return the vegetables to the skillet. Mix well. Sprinkle the bean sauce over and stir-fry for another 2 minutes. ■ Reduce the heat. Stir in the eggs, salt and pepper until the eggs just start to set. Cool. The mixture should be moist. ■ Layer 2 sheets of the phyllo pastry together, spraying each with the cooking spray. Cut in half lengthwise. Then cut each half crosswise into 4. Repeat to make a total of 32. ■ Place 2 tsp. (10 mL) of the filling along the longer side. Roll up into a thin roll, tucking in the ends. Brush with the melted butter and sprinkle with the sesame seeds. Place the rolls on a greased baking sheet. ■ Bake in a 375°F (190°C) oven for 13 minutes or until golden.

One roll... Energy 46cal/194kJ; Fat 3.2g; Protein 2g; Carbohydrate 2g

Tortilla Roll-Ups

Slice while still cold. Skewer immediately.
Serve slightly chilled or at room temperature.
Makes 27, 1 inch (2.5 cm) roll-ups.

4 oz.	Light cream cheese, softened	125 g
2 tbsp.	Low-fat salad dressing (or mayonnaise)	30 mL
2 tsp.	Dijon mustard	10 mL
¼ cup	Finely chopped dill pickles, drained	60 mL
3	10 inch (25 cm) flour tortillas	3
8 oz.	Deli shaved beef, or minced cooked roast beef	250 g

■ Combine the softened cream cheese, salad dressing and mustard in a small bowl until smooth. Add the pickles and mix well.
■ Spread the cheese mixture over the tortillas to the edges. ■ Lay the shaved beef over the cheese mixture or, if using cooked beef, sprinkle the minced beef over top. ■ Roll up the tortillas very tightly and wrap in plastic wrap. Refrigerate for at least 1 hour or overnight.
■ To serve, slice the chilled rolls into 1 inch (2.5 cm) pieces and skewer with a cocktail pick or toothpick.

One roll-up… Energy 46cal/191kJ;
Fat 1.2g; Protein 4g; Carbohydrate 3g

Beef and Herb Pinwheels

Freeze after baking. Reheat frozen pinwheels in a 350°F (175°C) oven for 20 to 30 minutes. Makes 30 hot appetizers.

2 cups	Biscuit mix	500 mL
¼ cup	Chopped fresh parsley	60 mL
½ cup	Water	125 mL
5 oz.	Garlic herb cream cheese, softened	150 g
½ lb.	Cooked lean beef, finely chopped, (or cooked lean ground beef)	225 g

■ Combine the biscuit mix and parsley. Add the water and stir to make a moist dough. Turn out onto a surface sprinkled lightly with additional biscuit mix. Knead 8 to 10 times. Roll out to a 11 x 15 inch (28 x 38 cm) rectangle ¼ inch (6 mm) thick. ■ Spread with the cream cheese and sprinkle evenly with the beef to within 1 inch (2.5 cm) of the edges. Roll up tightly starting from long edge. Seal the seam by pinching it closed. Slice into ½ inch (12 mm) slices and place on a lightly greased baking sheet. ■ Bake in a 425°F (220°C) oven for 10 to 15 minutes.

One appetizer… Energy 78cal/328kJ; Fat 3.6g; Protein 3g; Carbohydrate 8g

Beef Jerky

Store in an airtight container in the refrigerator or freeze for long-term storage. Makes ½ lb (225 g) jerky.

1 lb.	Lean flank, top round, or sirloin tip steak	454 g

MARINADE

¼ cup	Soy sauce	60 mL
2 tbsp.	Brown sugar	30 mL
1 tbsp.	Worcestershire sauce	15 mL
½ tsp.	Ground ginger	2 mL
½ tsp.	Salt	2 mL
⅛ tsp.	Pepper	0.5 mL

■ Cut the beef into ¼ inch (6 mm) strips.
■ Combine the 6 marinade ingredients in a small bowl. Mix well. Dip each beef strip into the marinade and place in a deep container. Pour the remaining marinade over all. Cover and refrigerate for 6 to 12 hours, turning several times. ■ Place a wire cooling rack on a baking sheet and lay a single layer of beef strips on the rack. ■ Place in a 175°F (80°C) oven for about 8 hours or until the beef is dried.

1/2 lb. (225 g) jerky… Energy 649cal/2715kJ; Fat 24.6g; Protein 92g; Carbohydrate 9g

Beef Snacks

Quick and easy. Uses leftover cooked beef. Reheat in the oven not in the microwave. Makes 16 appetizers.

½ cup	Cooked lean beef, thinly sliced and cut in strips	125mL
½ cup	Grated sharp Cheddar cheese	125 mL
1 tsp.	Dill weed	5 mL
7 oz.	Refrigerated crescent rolls	235 g
2 tbsp.	Cornmeal	30 mL

■ Mix the beef, cheese and dill together in a small bowl.
■ Separate the crescent dough into 8 triangles. Cut each triangle in half to make 16. Sprinkle the cornmeal on a cutting board and press the triangles into the cornmeal.
■ Place 1 tbsp. (15 mL) of the beef mixture onto the wide end of each triangle. Roll the triangle around the filling, pressing edges of dough to seal edges. Place on a lightly greased baking sheet. ■ Bake in a 375°F (190°C) oven for 12 to 15 minutes or until golden brown. Serve warm or cold.

One appetizer… Energy 73cal/304kJ; Fat 2.6g; Protein 4g; Carbohydrate 8g

CHAPTER 3

Barbecue

Teriyaki Burgers, page 38

Beef Souvlaki

Serve these with rice and a Greek salad. Serves 4.

1 lb.	Inside or outside round, sirloin tip or blade steak	454 g

MARINADE

¼ cup	Lemon juice	60 mL
2 tbsp.	Olive oil	30 mL
2	Large garlic cloves, minced	2
1 tbsp.	Fresh rosemary leaves	15 mL
1 tsp.	Dried oregano	5 mL
¼ tsp.	Freshly ground pepper	1 mL

YOGURT SAUCE

¼ tsp.	Salt	1 mL
½ cup	Peeled and grated cucumber	125 mL
½ cup	Plain yogurt	125 mL
2 tbsp.	Finely chopped fresh parsley	30 mL
2	Garlic cloves, minced	2
½ tsp.	Granulated sugar	2 mL
½ tsp.	Salt	2 mL

■ Cut the beef into 1 inch (2.5 cm) cubes and place in a small bowl or sealable plastic bag. Combine the 6 marinade ingredients and pour over the beef. Cover or seal. Marinate in the refrigerator for 4 hours or overnight, turning several times. ■ Remove the beef, discarding the marinade. Thread the beef cubes onto metal skewers, leaving a small space between each cube. ■ Barbecue the skewers over medium heat for 10 to 15 minutes or to desired doneness, turning often to brown evenly.

■ Sprinkle the first amount of salt over the cucumber in a small strainer. Allow to drain for 15 minutes. Blot dry with paper towels and combine in a small bowl with the remaining ingredients. Serve as a dip for the cubes.

One serving… 179cal/750kJ; Fat 6.5g; Protein 24g; Carbohydrate 5g

Taco 'Cheese' Burgers

Make and freeze the single patties ahead of time. Fully defrost before adding the cheese and doubling up. Serves 4.

BURGERS

1 lb.	Lean ground beef	454 g
¼ cup	Dry bread crumbs	60 mL
1	Large egg, beaten	1
1	Small onion, minced	1
1 tbsp.	Chili powder	15 mL
½ tsp.	Dry mustard powder	2 mL
½ tsp.	Salt	2 mL
	Freshly ground pepper, to taste	
4	Thin slices Monterey Jack cheese	4
4	Hamburger buns, split	4

GARNISH

Salsa

Sour cream

■ Combine the 8 burger ingredients in a medium bowl. Mix well. Shape into 8 thin patties. ■ Place a cheese slice on 4 of the patties and top with the remaining patties. Pinch the edges to seal. ■ Barbecue the patties over medium-high heat for 6 to 8 minutes per side or until no longer pink inside. Place the buns, cut side down, on the grill and toast to a light brown. ■ Garnish with your favorite salsa or sour cream.

One serving… Energy 440cal/1841kJ; Fat 20g; Protein 32g; Carbohydrate 32g

Beer Burgers

Serve burgers topped with onion mixture in buns. Makes 8 burgers.

BURGERS

2 lbs.	Lean ground beef	900 g
½ cup	Canned or bottled beer	125 mL
1	Large egg, fork-beaten	1
¼ cup	Dry bread crumbs	60 mL
1 tbsp.	Dry onion soup mix	15 mL
½ tsp.	Salt	2 mL
½ tsp.	Pepper	2 mL

TOPPING

2	Medium onions, sliced	2
2 tbsp.	Hard margarine	30 mL
½ cup	Canned or bottled beer	125 mL

■ Combine the 7 burger ingredients in a large bowl. Mix well. Shape into 8 patties, about ¾ inch (1.8 cm) thick. ■ Barbecue the burgers over medium-high heat for 5 minutes per side or until the center is no longer pink. ■ Sauté the onion in the margarine in a small non-stick skillet until soft. Stir in the beer and heat. Serve the burgers topped with the onion mixture in buns.

One serving… Energy 250cal/1045kJ; Fat 13.2g; Protein 22g; Carbohydrate 7g

Green Pepper Burgers

Make twice as many burgers. Barbecue and freeze extras for a quick dinner. Serves 6.

BURGERS

1½ lbs.	Lean ground beef	680 g
¾ cup	Soda cracker crumbs	175 mL
1	Large egg	1
½ cup	Skim evaporated milk	125 mL
¼ cup	Very finely chopped onion	60 mL
¾ cup	Very finely chopped green pepper	175 mL
1½ tsp.	Dry mustard powder	7 mL
1½ tsp.	Salt	7 mL
¼ tsp.	Pepper	1 mL
6	Canned pineapple slices, drained	6
2 tbsp.	Soy sauce	30 mL
6	Lettuce leaves	6
6	Kaiser buns, split	6

■ Combine the 9 burger ingredients in a large bowl. Mix together well. Form into 6 patties. Barbecue over medium-low heat for 5 to 6 minutes per side or until no longer pink in the center. Blot the pineapple rings on paper towels. Brush them with the soy sauce and barbecue 2 to 3 minutes per side.

■ Place a lettuce leaf on the bottom half of each kaiser bun. Top with a burger, a pineapple slice and the top half of the bun.

One serving… Energy 436cal/1824kJ; Fat 13.4g; Protein 30g; Carbohydrate 47g

Teriyaki Burgers

Top burgers with grilled pineapple slices. Serve in split and toasted buns. Makes 4 burgers.

¼ cup	Reserved pineapple juice	60 mL
3 tbsp.	Bottled steak sauce	50 mL
2 tbsp.	Soy sauce	30 mL
1½ tsp.	Freshly grated gingerroot	7 mL
1½ tsp.	Toasted sesame seeds	7 mL
1 lb.	Lean ground beef	454 g
1 cup	Bean sprouts, chopped	250 mL
2	Green onions, thinly sliced	2
8 oz.	Canned pineapple slices, juice reserved	227 mL

■ Combine the first 5 ingredients in a small bowl. Measure and pour ¼ cup (60 mL) of the sauce into a medium bowl. Set aside the remaining sauce. Add the ground beef, bean sprouts and green onion to the sauce in the medium bowl. Mix well. Form into 4 even-sized burgers. Barbecue over medium heat for 5 to 7 minutes per side or until no longer pink in the center, brushing often with the remaining sauce. ■ Barbecue the pineapple slices for 2 to 3 minutes per side.

One burger… Energy 238cal/995kJ; Fat 10.2g; Protein 23g; Carbohydrate 14g

Barbecued Fajitas

Keep beef more rare than well done as flank steak is most tender that way. Makes 8 fajitas.

MARINADE

¼ cup	Lime juice	60 mL
1 tbsp.	Olive oil	15 mL
1 tbsp.	Dried oregano	15 mL
½ tsp.	Crushed chilies	2 mL
¼ tsp.	Salt	1 mL
⅛ tsp.	Freshly ground pepper	0.5 mL
2	Garlic cloves, crushed	2
1½ lbs.	Flank steak	680 g
8	Flour tortillas, 8 inch (20 cm)	8

GARNISHES

Black Bean Salsa, page 14
Chopped tomatoes
Shredded lettuce
Sliced avocados
Sliced hot peppers
Sliced green onions

■ Combine the 7 marinade ingredients and pour over the steak. Place the steak in a shallow dish or sealable plastic bag. Turn to coat. Cover or seal. Marinate in the refrigerator overnight, turning several times. ■ Remove the steak, discarding the marinade. Barbecue over medium heat for 5 to 7 minutes per side for medium or to desired doneness. Slice the steak diagonally across the grain into thin slices. ■ Wrap the tortillas in foil. Heat until warmed but still soft. Fill with the sliced steak and selected garnishes.

One fajita... Energy 265cal/1107kJ;
Fat 7.2g; Protein 23g; Carbohydrate 25g

Grilled Steak and Vegetables

Vegetables may need to be done in 2 batches. Mushrooms will seem big but will shrink when cooked. Serves 6.

2	Medium zucchini, sliced ½ inch (12 mm) thick	2
1	Medium red onion, cut into wedges	1
1	Red pepper, cut into wedges	1
1	Yellow pepper, cut into wedges	1
18-20	Large fresh mushrooms	18-20
¾ cup	Low-fat Italian dressing	175 mL
2 tbsp.	Brown sugar	30 mL
1 tbsp.	Olive oil	15 mL
2 tsp.	Freshly ground pepper	10 mL
1 tsp.	Dry mustard powder	5 mL
1 tsp.	Ground coriander	5 mL
1 tsp.	Salt	5 mL
3	Garlic cloves, crushed	3
2 lbs.	Top sirloin, flank or top round steak, 1-1¼ inch (2.5-3 cm) thick	900 g

■ Combine the vegetables with the Italian dressing in a large bowl. Cover and marinate for 2 to 3 hours, stirring occasionally. ■ Combine the next 7 ingredients in a small bowl. Mix well. Spread over both sides of the steak. Barbecue over medium-low heat for 7 to 10 minutes per side for medium or to desired doneness. Keep the steaks warm on the warming rack of the barbecue or wrap in foil while cooking the vegetables. ■ Drain the vegetables. Place in a barbecue grilling pan. Barbecue over medium heat for 8 to 10 minutes or until tender-crisp and starting to brown, stirring occasionally. ■ Cut the steak diagonally across the grain into thin slices. Serve with the grilled vegetables.

One serving… 259cal/1082kJ;
Fat 8.6g; Protein 32g; Carbohydrate 13g

Spanish Sirloin

Serve thin slices either warm or cold with Aïoli Sauce, page 13. Serves 4.

2 tbsp.	Paprika	30 mL
4	Garlic cloves, minced	4
2 tbsp.	Lemon juice	30 mL
1 tsp.	Freshly ground pepper	5 mL
2 lbs.	Sirloin steak, 1 inch (2.5 cm) thick	900 g

■ Mix the paprika, garlic, lemon juice and pepper together in a small bowl. Spread the mixture on both sides of the steak. ■ Barbecue over medium heat for 8 to 10 minutes per side for medium or to desired doneness. Let stand 8 to 10 minutes. Slice thinly across the grain.

One serving… 281cal/1177kJ; Fat 8.7g; Protein 45g; Carbohydrate 4g

Holiday Steak

Serve the steaks with the hot marinade and Pineapple Salsa, page 14. Serves 6.

2 lbs.	Top sirloin, strip loin or rib steaks, ¾-1 inch (2-2.5 cm) thick	900 g
1	Garlic clove, cut in half	1

MARINADE

⅔ cup	Steak sauce (try spicy for extra zip)	150 mL
½ cup	Pineapple juice	125 mL
1	Lime, grated peel and juice	1
½ tsp.	Dried oregano	2 mL
½ tsp.	Ground cumin	2 mL
¼ tsp.	Cayenne pepper	1 mL

■ Rub both sides of the steaks with the cut sides of the garlic clove. Place the steaks in a shallow dish or sealable plastic bag. ■ Combine the 6 marinade ingredients and pour over the steaks. Turn to coat. Cover or seal. Marinate in the refrigerator for 20 to 30 minutes, turning once. ■ Remove the steaks, reserving the marinade. ■ Barbecue over medium-high heat for 5 to 7 minutes per side for medium or to desired doneness, basting often with the reserved marinade. Heat any remaining marinade to a boil. Simmer for 5 minutes.

One serving… Energy 210cal/879kJ; Fat 5.9g; Protein 31g; Carbohydrate 7g

Sizzling Barbecued Steak

Thicken the marinade with 1 tbsp. (15 mL) cornstarch and serve for those who enjoy horseradish flavor. Serves 6.

1½ lbs.	Blade, round or cross-rib steak	680 g

MARINADE

½ cup	Soy sauce	125 mL
⅓ cup	Prepared horseradish	75 mL
¼ cup	Red wine vinegar	60 mL
¼ cup	Lemon juice	60 mL
2 tbsp.	Vegetable oil	30 mL
2 tbsp.	Worcestershire sauce	30 mL
1 tbsp.	Finely chopped fresh parsley	15 mL
1 tbsp.	Dry mustard powder	15 mL
2	Garlic cloves, minced	2

■ Pierce the steak several times with a fork. Place in a shallow dish or sealable plastic bag.
■ Combine the 9 marinade ingredients and pour over the steak. Turn to coat. Cover or seal. Marinate in the refrigerator for 12 hours or overnight, turning several times. ■ Remove the steak, reserving the marinade. Barbecue over medium heat for 7 to 8 minutes per side for medium or to desired doneness, basting often with the marinade. Discard any remaining marinade.

One serving… Energy 155cal/649kJ;
Fat 8.3g; Protein 17g; Carbohydrate 3g

South Pacific Blade Steak

End result is tender and juicy. Ready in 25 minutes. Serves 4.

MARINADE

½ cup	Soy sauce	125 mL
¼ cup	Brown sugar, packed	60 mL
½ cup	White vinegar	125 mL
½ cup	Pineapple juice	125 mL
1	Large garlic clove, minced	1
1½ lbs.	Boneless blade steak, 1-1¼ inch (2.5-3 cm) thick	680 g
1 tbsp.	Cornstarch	15 mL

■ Combine the 5 marinade ingredients in a small saucepan. Bring to a boil. Simmer for 2 minutes. Cool. ■ Pierce the steak several times with a fork. Place in a shallow dish or sealable plastic bag. Pour the cooled marinade over the steak. Turn to coat. Cover or seal. Marinate in the refrigerate for 8 hours or overnight, turning several times. Remove the steak, reserving the marinade. ■ Barbecue over medium heat for 7 to 8 minutes per side for medium or until desired doneness. ■ Pour the marinade into a saucepan. Stir in the cornstarch. Boil and stir for 3 to 5 minutes until thickened. Serve over the steak.

One serving… Energy 281cal/1174kJ;
Fat 8.6g; Protein 25g; Carbohydrate 26g

Salsa-Stuffed Steak

The hotter the salsa the hotter the surprise. Prepare in 10 minutes. Serves 4.

1½ lbs.	Sirloin, strip loin, or rib-eye steak, ¾-1 inch (2-2.5 cm) thick	680 g
½ cup	Salsa (mild, medium or hot)	125 mL
2	Garlic cloves, minced	2
1	Small onion, finely chopped	1
1 tsp.	Ground cumin or dried oregano	5 mL
1 tsp.	Pepper	5 mL

GARNISH

Salsa (mild, medium or hot)
Sour cream

■ Cut the steak into 6 equal portions. Cut a deep horizontal pocket into 1 side of each steak. Combine the salsa, garlic and onion in a small bowl. Stuff the salsa mixture into each pocket and close the opening with a skewer. Season the steaks with the cumin and pepper. ■ Barbecue over medium-low heat for 5 to 7 minutes per side for medium or to desired doneness. ■ Garnish each portion with more salsa and sour cream, if desired.

One serving… Energy 224cal/937kJ;
Fat 6.4g; Protein 35g; Carbohydrate 6g

Citrus Steaks

From start to finish in 30 minutes.
Serves 4.

SAUCE

½ cup	Prepared orange juice	125 mL
⅓ cup	Ketchup	75 mL
¼ cup	Lemon juice	60 mL
¼ cup	Liquid honey	60 mL
2 tsp.	Dry mustard powder	10 mL
1 tsp.	Worcestershire sauce	5 mL
1 tsp.	Grated orange peel	5 mL
½ tsp.	Paprika	2 mL
1	Garlic clove, minced	1
	Salt, to taste	
	Pepper, to taste	

4	Rib-eye or strip loin steaks	4

■ Combine the 11 sauce ingredients in a small saucepan. Bring to a boil. Reduce the heat and simmer for 10 minutes or until the sauce is reduced to ¾ cup (175 mL).

■ Barbecue the steaks over medium heat for 2 minutes per side. Continue to barbecue for 4 to 5 minutes on each side for medium, or to desired doneness, brushing occasionally with the sauce.

■ Reheat any remaining sauce to boiling and serve over the steaks.

One serving… Energy 332cal/1390kJ;
Fat 9.7g; Protein 33g; Carbohydrate 29g

Tender and Tasty Beef Roast

All the preparation is done the day before. Only 40 minutes for cooking on serving day. Serves 10.

3½ lbs.	Boneless blade or cross-rib roast	1.6 kg

MARINADE

3 tbsp.	Olive oil	50 mL
½ cup	Dry red wine	125 mL
2 tbsp.	Chili sauce	30 mL
1	Garlic clove, minced	1
½ tsp.	Dry mustard powder	2 mL
½ tsp.	Lemon pepper	2 mL

■ Pierce the roast on both sides with a long-tined fork or skewer. Place in a large bowl or sealable plastic bag. ■ Combine the 6 marinade ingredients and pour over the roast. Turn to coat. Cover or seal. Marinate in the refrigerator for 12 hours or more, turning several times to coat. Remove the beef, reserving the marinade for basting. ■ Barbecue, using the indirect cooking method, over medium heat for 45 minutes per lb. (100 minutes per kg) or to desired doneness. Meat thermometer should register 160°F (70°C) for medium. Brush with the reserved marinade while barbecuing. Discard any remaining marinade.

One serving… Energy 193cal/807kJ; Fat 11.2g; Protein 19g; Carbohydrate 1g

Peppercorn Roast

Serve the horseradish sauce on the side.
Serves 10.

3½ lbs.	Inside round, rump or sirloin tip roast	1.6 kg
2 tsp.	Crushed peppercorns	10 mL
½ tsp.	Ground cloves	2 mL
½ tsp.	Dried oregano	2 mL
2 tbsp.	Dijon mustard	30 mL
1 tbsp.	Lemon juice	15 mL

HORSERADISH SAUCE

1 cup	Sour cream	250 mL
1 tbsp.	Grated fresh horseradish, drained	15 mL
1 tbsp.	Dijon mustard	15 mL
1 tsp.	Lemon juice	5 mL
	Salt, to taste	
	Pepper, to taste	

■ Place the roast in a large bowl. Combine the pepper, cloves, oregano, mustard and lemon juice and rub over all surfaces of the roast. Cover and refrigerate overnight. ■ Barbecue, using the indirect cooking method, over medium heat for 35 minutes per lb. (75 minutes per kg) for rare or 45 minutes per lb. (100 minutes per kg) for medium doneness. ■ Combine the 6 sauce ingredients in a small bowl and mix well.

One serving… Energy 223cal/933kJ;
Fat 10.3g; Protein 29g; Carbohydrate 2g

Barbecued Beef Ribs

Serve remaining sauce over rice or mashed potatoes. Serves 6.

4 lbs.	Beef back ribs	1.8 kg
3 tbsp.	Water	50 mL
	Freshly ground pepper, to taste	

BARBECUE SAUCE

1 cup	Chili sauce	250 mL
7½ oz.	Tomato sauce	213 mL
2	Garlic cloves, crushed	2
1 tsp.	Brown sugar	5 mL
1 tsp.	Hot pepper sauce	5 mL
2 tbsp.	Dijon mustard	30 mL
1 tbsp.	Lemon juice	15 mL
1 tsp.	Crushed chilies	5 mL

■ Divide the ribs onto two large sheets of heavy duty aluminum foil (or double layers of regular foil). Sprinkle with the water and pepper. Bring the long sides of the foil up over the ribs and fold together. Crease to seal the top. Press the short sides of the foil together at each end. Fold to seal each packet well. Barbecue each packet over low heat for 1½ hours, turning 5 times or every 18 to 20 minutes. ■ Combine the 8 sauce ingredients in a saucepan. Bring to a boil. Reduce the heat and simmer, uncovered, for 10 to 15 minutes until the sauce is slightly reduced and thickened. ■ Remove the beef ribs from the foil and place directly on the grill over medium heat. Brush the ribs well with the sauce. Barbecue for 10 minutes, or until browned and glazed, turning and basting once.

One serving... Energy 402cal/1681kJ;
Fat 20.1g; Protein 39g; Carbohydrate 16g

Orange-Glazed BBQ Ribs

Watch these carefully while barbecuing as they will burn easily because of the sugars in the marinade. Serves 6.

| 4 lbs. | Beef ribs, individually cut (about 10 to 12) | 1.8 kg |

MARINADE

¾ cup	Burgundy wine	175 mL
½ cup	Vegetable oil	125 mL
¾ cup	Orange marmalade	175 mL
¼ cup	Soy sauce	60 mL
1	Garlic clove, minced	1
2 tbsp.	Freshly grated gingerroot	30 mL
2 tsp.	Dry mustard powder	10 mL
1 tsp.	Salt	5 mL
½ tsp.	Pepper	2 mL

■ Place the rib bones in a shallow dish or sealable plastic bag. ■ Combine the 9 marinade ingredients and pour over the ribs. Turn to coat. Cover or seal. Marinate in the refrigerator overnight, turning several times. ■ Remove the ribs, reserving the marinade for basting. Barbecue over medium-low heat for 30 to 40 minutes or until tender, turning and brushing frequently with the marinade. Discard any remaining marinade.

One serving… 420cal/1756kJ; Fat 25.3g; Protein 30g; Carbohydrate 15g

Peppered Beef Skewers

Use 6, 8 inch (20 cm) bamboo skewers soaked in water for 10 minutes. Cut the beef into about 36 cubes. Makes 6 kabobs.

1 tbsp.	Olive oil	15 mL
½ tsp.	Dijon mustard	2 mL
1 lb.	Sirloin steak, cut into 1 inch (2.5 cm) cubes	454 g
2 tbsp.	Freshly ground pepper	30 mL

■ Combine the olive oil and mustard in a small bowl. Stir well. Brush the mustard mixture on the beef cubes. Roll each cube lightly in the pepper. Push 6 cubes onto 1 presoaked bamboo skewer. Repeat for the remaining 5 skewers.

■ Barbecue over medium heat for 4 to 5 minutes. Turn. Continue cooking for another 4 to 5 minutes or to desired doneness.

One kabob… Energy 115cal/480kJ; Fat 5.1g; Protein 15g; Carbohydrate 1g

Beef Kabobs with Oregano and Onion

Only 15 minutes to assemble. Makes 5 kabobs.

1 lb.	Inside or top round or blade steak, cut into 20, 1 inch (2.5 cm) cubes	454 g

MARINADE

1	Garlic clove, minced	1
1 tsp.	Salt	5 mL
⅓ cup	Olive oil	75 mL
⅓ cup	Dry red wine	75 mL
¼ cup	Red wine vinegar	60 mL
Dash	Hot pepper sauce	Dash
1 tbsp.	Dried oregano	15 mL
15	Pickled onions	15
15	Fresh mushrooms	15
2	Red peppers, cut into 15, 2 inch (5 cm) chunks	2

■ Place the beef cubes in a medium bowl or sealable plastic bag. Combine the 7 marinade ingredients and pour over the beef. Cover or seal. Marinate in the refrigerator overnight, turning several times. ■ Leave at room temperature for 1 hour before barbecuing. Remove the beef, reserving the marinade for basting.

■ Skewer 4 pieces of beef alternately with 3 onions, 3 mushrooms and 3 red pepper chunks. Repeat for 4 more skewers. Baste with the marinade. Barbecue over medium heat for 6 to 8 minutes, turning and basting often. Discard any remaining marinade.

One serving… Energy 232cal/828kJ; Fat 7.2g; Protein 21g; Carbohydrate 12g

Kabob Sauces

Alternate cubes of beef and your favorite vegetables on skewers. Marinate beef ahead of time, if desired. Use marinade or glaze to baste kabobs while barbecuing.

CARIBBEAN MARINADE

Makes 1½ cups (375 mL) marinade.

1 cup	Pineapple juice	250 mL
1	Lime, grated peel and juice	1
1	Small onion, finely chopped	1
2	Garlic cloves, minced	2
1 tsp.	Chopped gingerroot	5 mL
¼ tsp.	Hot pepper sauce	1 mL

■ Combine all 6 ingredients. Marinate beef for 4 hours or overnight.

One recipe… Energy 201cal/843kJ; Fat 0.4g; Protein 2g; Carbohydrate 50g

TERIYAKI MARINADE

Makes ½ cup (125 mL) marinade.

¼ cup	Soy sauce	60 mL
2 tbsp.	Water	30 mL
2 tbsp.	Liquid honey	30 mL
1	Small garlic clove, minced	1
⅛ tsp.	Ground ginger	0.5 mL

■ Combine all 5 ingredients. Simmer for 5 minutes.

One recipe… Energy 180cal/755kJ; Fat trace; Protein 7g; Carbohydrate 42g

GOLDEN GLAZE

Makes 1 cup (250 mL) glaze.

1 tbsp.	Beef bouillon powder	15 mL
1 tbsp.	Dry onion flakes	15 mL
⅔ cup	Apricot jam	150 mL
½ cup	Water	125 mL
½ tsp.	Ground ginger	2 mL

■ Combine all 5 ingredients. Simmer for 5 minutes. Barbecue kabobs basting with the glaze several times.

One recipe… Energy 601cal/2512kJ; Fat 1.2g; Protein 4g; Carbohydrate 150g

Thai Beef Kabobs

Use 8, 10 inch (25 cm) bamboo skewers soaked in water for 10 minutes. Serves 4.

1 lb.	Top sirloin or inside round steak, 1 inch (2.5 cm) thick	454 g

PINEAPPLE PEANUT SAUCE

½ cup	Steak sauce	125 mL
½ cup	Reserved pineapple juice	125 mL
2 tbsp.	Chunky-style peanut butter	30 mL
1 tbsp.	Soy sauce	15 mL
1 tbsp.	Brown sugar	15 mL
1-2 tsp.	Crushed chilies	5-10 mL
½ tsp.	Curry powder	2 mL
2	Garlic cloves, crushed	2
1	Whole firm cantaloupe	1
1	Large green pepper	1
14 oz.	Canned pineapple chunks, juice reserved	398 mL

■ Cut the steak into thin strips ¼ inch (6 mm) thick and 5 inches (12.5 cm) long. Place in a medium bowl or sealable plastic bag. Combine the 8 sauce ingredients and pour over the beef strips into the sauce. Cover or seal. Marinate in the refrigerator for 20 to 30 minutes. ■ Cut the cantaloupe and green pepper into uniform chunks. Thread the beef onto the presoaked bamboo skewers, alternating the pineapple, cantaloupe and pepper chunks between the folds of the beef. Barbecue 6 to 8 minutes over medium heat, turning and brushing often with the sauce. Bring the remaining sauce to a boil and simmer for 5 minutes. Use as a dipping sauce for the beef.

One serving… Energy 310cal/1298kJ;
Fat 9.2g; Protein 28g; Carbohydrate 31g

Hawaiian Kabobs

Serve these on a bed of rice. Serves 4.

1 lb.	Sirloin tip or round steak, cut in 12,1½ inch (3.8 cm) cubes	454 g

MARINADE

½ cup	Reserved pineapple juice	125 mL
1 tbsp.	Soy sauce	15 mL
¼ cup	Brown sugar, packed	60 mL
¼ cup	White vinegar	60 mL
1 tbsp.	Cornstarch	15 mL
3 tbsp.	Water	50 mL
14 oz.	Canned pineapple chunks, juice reserved	398 mL
½	Green pepper, cut into 8 chunks	½
8	Large fresh mushrooms	8
8	Large cherry tomatoes	8

■ Place the beef cubes in a medium bowl or sealable plastic bag. ■ Combine the 4 marinade ingredients and pour over the beef. ■ Cover or seal. Marinate in the refrigerator for 6 to 8 hours or overnight, turning several times. ■ Drain the marinade into a small saucepan. Mix the cornstarch with the water and stir into the marinade. Heat to thicken. ■ Alternate the beef cubes, pineapple chunks, green pepper chunks, mushrooms and tomatoes on 4 metal skewers. Barbecue over medium-low heat for 6 to 8 minutes or to desired doneness, turning and basting every 2 minutes with the sauce. Discard any remaining marinade.

One serving… Energy 278cal/1164kJ;
Fat 4.5g; Protein 24g; Carbohydrate 37g

BBQ Party Salad

Invite guests early and have them cut and chop
while you barbecue. Serves 8.

2 lbs.	Sirloin steak, 1½ inch (3.8 cm) thick	900 g
2 tbsp.	Dijon mustard	30 mL
1 tsp.	Freshly ground pepper	5 mL
2	Ears of corn, husked	2
3 tbsp.	Olive oil	50 mL
3	Green, red, or yellow peppers	3
2	Medium zucchini, with peel, sliced in half lengthwise	2
2	Red onions, sliced into ¼ inch (6 mm) rings	2
2	Tomatoes, diced	2
½ cup	Sliced pitted ripe olives	125 mL

DRESSING

3 tbsp.	Balsamic or red wine vinegar	50 mL
2	Garlic cloves, minced	2
1½ tsp.	Salt	7 mL
½ tsp.	Pepper	2 mL
⅓ cup	Olive oil	75 mL
3 tbsp.	Chopped fresh parsley	50 mL
3 tbsp.	Chopped chives or green onion	50 mL
4 cups	Mixed chopped salad greens	1 L

■ Pat the steak dry with a paper towel. Combine the mustard and pepper and spread on both sides of the steak. Barbecue over medium-hot heat for 8 to 10 minutes per side for medium or to desired doneness. Cover with foil and let stand while barbecuing the vegetables.

■ Brush the corn with some of the first amount of oil. Barbecue over medium heat, turning until the kernels start to crackle and are lightly golden. Cool slightly. Cut the kernels off the cob with a sharp knife. Place in a very large bowl. ■ Barbecue the whole peppers over high heat until blackened. Place in a bowl and cover with plastic wrap or in a paper bag and close. When cooled enough to handle, peel and discard the skin. Cut in half and remove the seeds and white ribs. Dice and combine with the corn kernels. ■ Brush the zucchini slices with more of the oil and barbecue over medium heat until golden. Dice and add to the bowl. Repeat with the onion slices. ■ Add the diced tomatoes and olives. ■ Combine the vinegar with the garlic, salt and pepper. Whisk in the second amount of oil. Add the parsley and chives. Toss with the barbecued vegetables.

■ Cut the steak diagonally across the grain into thin slices. Slice crosswise into 1 inch (2.5 cm) strips. Toss with the vegetables in the bowl.

■ Add the salad greens and toss to mix.

One serving… Energy 324cal/1353kJ;
Fat 19.6g; Protein 25g; Carbohydrate 14g

CHAPTER 4

Casseroles

Taco on a Platter, page 62

Sloppy Joe Pasta Casserole

Preparation time 20 minutes. Serves 8.

2 cups	Ziti or penne pasta, uncooked	500 mL
1½ lbs.	Lean ground beef	680 g
1 cup	Diced onion	250 mL
1 cup	Diced green pepper	250 mL
1 tbsp.	Prepared mustard	15 mL
¼ cup	Brown sugar, packed	60 mL
2 tbsp.	Cider vinegar	30 mL
2 tbsp.	Worcestershire sauce	30 mL
28 oz.	Canned stewed tomatoes, with juice	796 mL
7½ oz.	Tomato sauce	213 mL
5½ oz.	Tomato paste	156 mL
½ tsp.	Ground allspice	2 mL
½ tsp.	Hot pepper sauce	2 mL
½ tsp.	Dried oregano	2 mL
1 tsp.	Salt	5 mL
¼ tsp.	Pepper	1 mL

■ Cook the pasta according to package directions. Drain and keep in cold water. ■ Scramble-fry the beef in a non-stick skillet for 5 minutes. Add the onion and green pepper and cook until the beef is browned and the onion is soft. Drain. ■ Add the remaining ingredients. Mix well. Bring the mixture to a boil. Cover and simmer for 20 minutes. Add the drained pasta and spoon into a lightly sprayed 9 x 13 inch (22 x 33 cm) pan or a 3 quart (3 L) casserole dish. Bake, uncovered, in a 350°F (175°C) oven for 20 minutes or until hot.

One serving… Energy 330cal/1379kJ;
Fat 8.0g; Protein 22g; Carbohydrates 44g

Potato-Topped Beef Casserole

Assemble the day before. Cover and refrigerate overnight. Bake 15 minutes longer if taking directly from the refrigerator. Serves 6.

6	Medium potatoes, cut in quarters	6
	Boiling water, to cover	
⅓ cup	1% milk	75 mL
1 tsp.	Salt	5 mL
¼ tsp.	Pepper	1 mL
1 lb.	Lean ground beef	454 g
½ cup	Chopped green onion	125 mL
7½ oz.	Tomato sauce	213 mL
½ tsp.	Dried sweet basil	2 mL
⅛ tsp.	Pepper	0.5 mL
12 oz.	Canned kernel corn, drained (or 1 cup, 250 mL frozen)	341 mL
½ cup	Grated medium or sharp Cheddar cheese	125 mL

■ Cook the potatoes in the boiling water until fork-tender. Drain. Add the milk, salt and first amount of pepper. Mash well. Set aside.

■ Scramble-fry the beef and onion in a non-stick skillet until the beef is no longer pink.

■ Mix the tomato sauce, basil and second amount of pepper in a small bowl. Stir well. Add to the beef mixture. Stir in the kernel corn. Mix well. Turn into a lightly sprayed 2 quart (2 L) casserole dish. Smooth the mixture. Spread the mashed potatoes over the beef layer. Smooth the top. Sprinkle with the cheese. ■ Bake, uncovered, in a 350°F (175°C) oven for 30 minutes. Let stand 5 minutes before serving.

One serving… Energy 307cal/1285kJ
Fat 10.2g; Protein 21g; Carbohydrate 35g

Rice and Meatballs

Chop the vegetables while the meatballs are browning. Serves 6.

1½ lbs.	Lean ground beef	680 g
½ cup	Dry bread crumbs	125 mL
¼ cup	1% milk	60 mL
1 tsp.	Salt	5 mL
1 tsp.	Dried thyme, crushed	5 mL
½ tsp.	Dried marjoram, crushed	2 mL
1	Large egg	1
1 tbsp.	Olive oil	15 mL
3	Large celery stalks, chopped	3
1	Large onion, chopped	1
1½ cups	Long grain white rice, uncooked	375 mL
2 tsp.	Beef bouillon powder	10 mL
1½ cups	Water	375 mL
28 oz.	Canned stewed tomatoes, with juice, coarsely chopped	796 mL
1	Large green pepper, chopped	1
1 tsp.	Ground thyme	5 mL
½ tsp.	Ground marjoram	2 mL

■ Combine the first 7 ingredients in a large bowl. Mix well. Form into 1½ inch (3.8 cm) balls. Brown evenly in a non-stick skillet. Drain. Remove the meatballs to a lightly sprayed medium roaster. ■ In the same skillet, heat the oil and sauté the celery, onion and rice until the vegetables are soft and the rice starts to brown. Remove to the roaster with the meatballs and add the remaining ingredients. ■ Bake, covered, in a 350°F (175°C) oven for 1½ hours or until the rice is tender.

One serving… Energy 482cal/2015kJ; Fat 13.8g; Protein 28g; Carbohydrate 60g

Spicy Italian Casserole

Prepare in 15 minutes. Ready in less than an hour. Serves 4.

¾ cup	Rotini or fusilli pasta, uncooked	175 mL
1 lb.	Sirloin steak, cut in 2½ x ¼ inch (6.4 x 0.6 cm) strips (or 2 cups, 500 mL cooked beef, cubed)	454 g
1 tsp.	Vegetable oil	5 mL
1	Small onion, chopped	1
½ cup	Chopped green pepper	125 mL
19 oz.	Canned stewed tomatoes, with juice, chopped	540 mL
7½ oz.	Tomato sauce	213 mL
3 tbsp.	All-purpose flour	50 mL
2 tsp.	Beef bouillon powder	10 mL
½ tsp.	Dried oregano	2 mL
¼ tsp.	Salt	1 mL
	Pepper, to taste	
	Grated part skim mozzarella cheese	

■ Cook the pasta according to package directions. Drain and keep in cold water while preparing the meat sauce. ■ Sauté the beef strips in the hot oil in a non-stick skillet for 5 minutes. Add the onion and green pepper and sauté until the onion is slightly soft. Add the tomatoes. ■ Combine the tomato sauce and flour in a small bowl and stir well. Add the tomato mixture, bouillon powder, oregano, salt and pepper to the beef. Boil and thicken, stirring often. ■ Spoon into an ungreased 1½ quart (1.5 L) casserole dish and combine with the drained cooked pasta. ■ Bake, uncovered, in a 350°F (175°C) oven for 30 minutes. ■ Sprinkle individual servings with mozzarella cheese.

One serving… Energy 296cal/1237kJ; Fat 6.1g; Protein 28g; Carbohydrate 33g

Company Chili

Make the day before to allow the flavors to blend. Serves 8.

2½ lbs.	Chuck steak or stewing beef, all visible fat and sinew removed	1.1 kg
1 tsp.	Vegetable oil	5 mL
1	Large onion, chopped	1
3	Celery ribs, chopped	3
1	Large green pepper, chopped	1
2	Garlic cloves, minced	2
2	Jalapeño peppers, diced (wear gloves)	2
28 oz.	Canned tomatoes, with juice, chopped	796 mL
5½ oz.	Tomato paste	156 mL
1 cup	Water	250 mL
1½ tbsp.	Chili powder	25 mL
1 tbsp.	Brown sugar	15 mL
1 tsp.	Salt	5 mL
⅛ tsp.	Pepper	0.5 mL
1 tsp.	Worcestershire sauce	5 mL
1 tbsp.	White vinegar	15 mL
2 x 14 oz.	Canned kidney beans, drained	2 x 398 mL

GARNISH

Grated medium Cheddar cheese
Red onion, diced

■ Cut the beef into ¾ inch (2 cm) cubes. Heat the oil in an ovenproof Dutch oven until hot. Add the beef cubes. Quickly brown on all sides. ■ Add the next 5 ingredients and continue to cook for 10 minutes, or until the vegetables are soft. ■ Add the next 10 ingredients. Stir well. Bring the mixture to a simmer. Cover. ■ Bake in a 325°F (160°C) oven for 1 hour or until the beef is tender. Remove the lid and continue to bake for 30 minutes. ■ Garnish individual servings with Cheddar cheese and red onion.

One serving… Energy 304cal/1270kJ; Fat 6.4g; Protein 33g; Carbohydrate 30g

Three Bean Chili

Add more chili powder for more zip. Serves 6.

1 lb.	Lean ground beef	454 g
1 cup	Chopped onion	250 mL
½ cup	Grated carrot	125 mL
1	Garlic clove, minced	1
1 tbsp.	Chili powder	15 mL
½ tsp.	Ground cumin	2 mL
14 oz.	Canned black beans, drained	398 mL
19 oz.	Canned romano beans, with liquid	540 mL
14 oz.	Canned kidney beans, with liquid	398 mL
28 oz.	Canned crushed tomatoes	796 mL
4 oz.	Canned diced green chilies, drained	114 mL

GARNISH

Chopped fresh cilantro (coriander)

■ Scramble-fry the beef, onion, carrot and garlic in a non-stick skillet until the beef is browned. Drain. ■ Add the chili powder and cumin. Stir well. Remove from the heat. ■ Combine the next 5 ingredients in a Dutch oven. Add the ground beef mixture and stir. ■ Cover and simmer for 1 hour, stirring often. ■ Garnish with cilantro.

One serving… Energy 383cal/1601kJ; Fat 7.7g; Protein 30g; Carbohydrate 50g

Easy Skillet Chili

Make a salad and defrost buns while chili is simmering. Serves 6.

1 lb.	Lean ground beef	454 g
1	Garlic clove, minced	1
1	Large onion, chopped	1
1	Large green pepper, chopped	1
2 cups	Sliced fresh mushrooms	500 mL
14 oz.	Canned tomatoes, with juice, chopped	398 mL
7½ oz.	Tomato sauce	213 mL
5½ oz.	Tomato paste	156 mL
14 oz.	Canned red kidney beans, with liquid	398 mL
1 tsp.	Salt	5 mL
2 tsp.	Chili powder	10 mL
1	Bay leaf	1

■ Scramble-fry the beef in a large non-stick skillet. Drain. ■ Add the next 4 ingredients and cook until the vegetables are soft. ■ Add the remaining 7 ingredients. Cover and simmer for 1 hour, stirring occasionally. Remove the bay leaf.

One serving… Energy 244cal/1020kJ; Fat 7.3g; Protein 21g; Carbohydrate 26g

Skillet Chili 'n' Pasta

Only a skillet and 15 minutes are needed to prepare this easy one-dish meal. Serves 4.

¾ lb.	Lean ground beef	340 g
1	Medium onion, diced	1
1	Garlic clove, minced	1
28 oz.	Canned stewed tomatoes, with juice, chopped	796 mL
1 cup	Tomato juice	250 mL
14 oz.	Canned kidney beans, with liquid	398 mL
1 tbsp.	Chili powder	15 mL
1 cup	Fusilli pasta, uncooked	250 mL
2 tbsp.	Chopped fresh sweet basil	30 mL

■ Scramble-fry the beef, onion and garlic in a non-stick skillet until the beef is browned and the onion is soft. Drain. ■ Add the next 4 ingredients and bring to a boil. ■ Add the uncooked pasta and basil and bring to a boil. Cover and simmer for 15 minutes or until the pasta is cooked.

One serving… Energy 383cal/1603kJ; Fat 8.4g; Protein 27g; Carbohydrate 53g

Chunky Chili

Addition of rice makes this a one-dish meal. Serve with salad and rolls. Serves 6.

1 lb.	Top round or sirloin tip steak, cut into ¾ inch (2 cm) cubes	454 g
1	Onion, chopped	1
1 tsp.	Vegetable oil	5 mL
2 x 14 oz.	Canned Mexican-style stewed tomatoes, with juice (see Note)	2 x 398 mL
14 oz.	Canned kidney beans, with liquid	398 mL
1	Green pepper, chopped	1
¾ cup	Long grain white rice, uncooked	175 mL
1 cup	Water	250 mL
1 tbsp.	Cocoa powder	15 mL
2 tsp.	Chili powder	10 mL
½ tsp.	Salt	2 mL

■ Brown the beef and onion in the oil in a large non-stick skillet. Stir in the remaining ingredients. Bring to a boil. ■ Cover and simmer for 1 hour or until the beef is tender and the rice is done.

Note: If Mexican or Chili-style stewed tomatoes are not available, substitute regular stewed tomatoes plus an additional 2 tsp. (10 mL) chili powder.

One serving… Energy 289cal/1208kJ; Fat 4.4g; Protein 22g; Carbohydrate 42g

61

Taco on a Platter

Make the meat sauce the day before. Cover and chill. Heat thoroughly just before assembling. Serves 12.

2 lbs.	Lean ground beef	900 g
1	Medium onion, chopped	1
13 oz.	Tomato paste	369 mL
14 oz.	Canned crushed tomatoes	398 mL
2 tbsp.	Chili powder	30 mL
1 tsp.	Ground cumin	5 mL
½ tsp.	Garlic powder	2 mL
2 tsp.	Salt	10 mL
28 oz.	Canned beans in tomato sauce, with liquid	796 mL
2 cups	Corn chips, broken	500 mL
2 cups	Hot cooked long grain white rice	500 mL
2 cups	Grated medium Cheddar cheese	500 mL
1	Medium red onion, chopped	1
1	Head iceberg lettuce, shredded	1
3	Medium tomatoes, chopped	3
⅓ cup	Sliced ripe pitted olives	75 mL
	Picante sauce or salsa	

■ Scramble-fry the beef and first amount of onion in a large non-stick skillet. Drain.
■ Add the next 6 ingredients. Mix well. Simmer, uncovered, for 15 minutes. ■ Add the beans. Heat through. ■ Layer the corn chips, rice, beef mixture, cheese, second amount of onion, lettuce, tomato and olives on a large platter. ■ Serve with picante sauce.

One serving… Energy 435cal/1819kJ; Fat 17.7g; Protein 27g; Carbohydrate 46g

Corned Beef and Sauerkraut Casserole

Easy 20 minute preparation. Use leftover mashed potatoes for an even quicker time. Serves 8.

6	Medium potatoes	6
	Boiling water, to cover	
½ cup	1% milk	125 mL
1 tbsp.	Hard margarine	15 mL
⅛ tsp.	Salt	0.5 mL
	Freshly ground pepper, to taste	
1 tbsp.	Hard margarine	15 mL
1	Medium onion, slivered	1
2 cups	Canned sauerkraut, rinsed and drained well	500 mL
3 cups	Sliced corned beef, cut into thin strips (or use deli corned beef)	750 mL
1 cup	Grated Swiss cheese	250 mL
	Paprika	
	Caraway seed	

■ Cook the potatoes in the boiling water until fork-tender. Drain. Add the milk, first amount of margarine, salt and pepper. Mash until smooth. Set aside. ■ Melt the second amount of margarine in a non-stick skillet. Add the onion and sauté for 5 minutes. Add the sauerkraut and sauté until the liquid is evaporated and the mixture is fairly dry. Combine with the mashed potatoes. ■ Spread ½ the potato mixture in a lightly sprayed 3 quart (3 L) casserole dish. Sprinkle with the corned beef and cheese. Cover with the rest of the potato mixture. Sprinkle with paprika and caraway seed. ■ Bake, uncovered, in a 350°F (175°C) oven for 30 to 45 minutes.

One serving… Energy 311cal/1303kJ;
Fat 17.9g; Protein 17g; Carbohydrate 21g

Traditional Lasagne

Assemble the day before. Cover and refrigerate. 70 minutes before serving remove from the refrigerator and bake, uncovered, in a 375°F (190°C) oven for 1 hour. Let stand 10 minutes before cutting. Serves 8.

12	Lasagne noodles (or 8 oz., 250 g pkg.)	12
1 lb.	Lean ground beef	454 g
1	Garlic clove, minced	1
1 cup	Chopped onion	250 mL
1 tsp.	Dried oregano	5 mL
½ tsp.	Pepper	2 mL
14 oz.	Canned stewed tomatoes, with juice, chopped	398 mL
5½ oz.	Tomato paste	156 mL
7½ oz.	Tomato sauce	213 mL
1½ cups	Dry curd cottage cheese	375 mL
1 cup	Grated part skim mozzarella cheese	250 mL
¼ cup	Grated Parmesan cheese	60 mL
1	Garlic clove, minced	1
1 tbsp.	Dried parsley flakes	15 mL
2 tsp.	Dried sweet basil	10 mL
½ tsp.	Salt	2 mL
2 cups	Grated part skim mozzarella cheese	500 mL
¼ cup	Grated Parmesan cheese	60 mL

■ Cook the lasagne noodles according to package directions. Drain. Let cool in cold water until ready to use. ■ Scramble-fry the beef, first amount of garlic and onion in a non-stick skillet until the beef is browned and the onion is soft. Drain. Add the oregano and pepper. Mix in the tomatoes, tomato paste and tomato sauce. Simmer for 10 minutes.

■ Combine the cottage cheese with the first amounts of mozzarella and Parmesan cheese, second amount of garlic, parsley flakes, basil and salt in a large bowl.

■ Spread about 1 cup (250 mL) of the sauce in the bottom of a lightly sprayed 9 x 13 inch (22 x 33 cm) pan. Lay 4 drained lasagne noodles over top. Cover with a layer of 1½ cups (375 mL) of the sauce and another layer of 4 noodles. Spread the cheese mixture over the noodles and cover with the remaining 4 noodles. Spread the remaining 1½ cups (375 mL) of sauce over top and cover with the second amounts of mozzarella and Parmesan cheese. ■ Cover with lightly sprayed foil. Bake in a 350°F (175°C) oven for 30 minutes. Remove the foil and continue baking for 15 minutes or until the cheese has browned slightly. Let stand 10 minutes before cutting.

One serving… Energy 423cal/1770kJ; Fat 14.9g; Protein 35g; Carbohydrate 37g

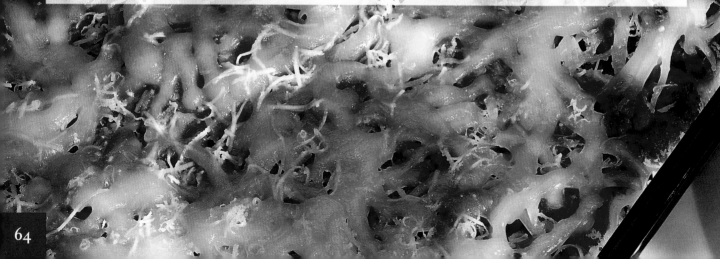

Mexican Lasagne

No need to cook the noodles ahead of time. Serves 8.

1 lb.	Lean ground beef	454 g
1	Medium onion, chopped	1
1	Garlic clove, minced	1
¼ cup	Chopped fresh cilantro (coriander)	60 mL
3 cups	Salsa (mild, medium or hot)	750 mL
1 tsp.	Chili powder	5 mL
7½ oz.	Tomato sauce	213 mL
1 cup	Water	250 mL
16 oz.	Part skim ricotta cheese	500 g
1	Large egg	1
½ tsp.	Salt	2 mL
¼ tsp.	Pepper	1 mL
12	Lasagne noodles, uncooked	12
2½ cups	Grated Monterey Jack cheese	625 mL

■ Scramble-fry the beef in a large non-stick skillet for 5 minutes. Add the onion, garlic and cilantro and cook until the beef is browned and onion is soft. Drain.
■ Add the salsa, chili powder, tomato sauce and water. Stir together until the salsa mixture comes to a boil.
■ Combine the ricotta cheese, egg, salt and pepper in a medium bowl. ■ Pour 1¼ cups (300 mL) of the salsa mixture into a lightly sprayed 9 x 13 inch (22 x 33 cm) pan. Spread evenly over the bottom. Cover with 4 uncooked lasagne noodles. Pour another 1¼ cups (300 mL) of salsa mixture over and add another layer of 4 noodles. Spread the ricotta mixture over and then add the remaining 4 noodles. Pour the remaining salsa mixture over all and sprinkle with the Jack cheese. ■ Cover the pan tightly with lightly sprayed foil. ■ Bake in a 350°F (175°C) oven for 1¼ hours. Remove the foil and continue baking for 15 minutes. Let stand 10 minutes before cutting.

One serving… Energy 479cal/2003kJ;
Fat 22.3g; Protein 33g; Carbohydrate 37g

65

Comfort Casserole

Serve this with green beans or a salad.
Serves 4.

2 lbs.	Lean ground beef	900 g
1 cup	Chopped onion	250 mL
1 cup	Chopped celery	250 mL
2	Large garlic cloves, minced	2
¼ tsp.	Pepper	1 mL
1½ cups	Sliced fresh mushrooms	375 mL
1 tbsp.	Beef bouillon powder	15 mL
2¼ cups	Boiling water	560 mL
¼ cup	Soy sauce	60 mL
1 cup	Long grain white rice, uncooked	250 mL

■ Scramble-fry the beef, onion, celery, garlic and pepper in a non-stick skillet until the beef is no longer pink. Drain. ■ Add the mushrooms. Sauté for 5 minutes. ■ Dissolve the bouillon powder in the boiling water. Add to the beef mixture. Mix well. ■ Stir in the soy sauce and rice. Simmer, covered, for 30 to 40 minutes or until the rice is tender.

One serving… Energy 567cal/2374kJ; Fat 19.4g; Protein 47g; Carbohydrate 48g

Beef and Rice Quiche

Do the roasted pepper ahead of time. Quiche cuts into 8 lunch size wedges.

2 cups	Warm cooked long grain white rice	500 mL
2 tbsp.	Chopped fresh chives	30 mL
1	Large egg	1
3	Large eggs, fork-beaten	3
13½ oz.	Skim evaporated milk	385 mL
½ cup	Sliced green onion	125 mL
1 tbsp.	Chopped fresh parsley	15 mL
½ tsp.	Liquid smoke	2 mL
½ tsp.	Salt	2 mL
½ tsp.	Dry mustard powder	2 mL
1 cup	Finely chopped cooked lean beef	250 mL
1 cup	Grated medium Cheddar cheese	250 mL
1	Red Roasted Pepper, page 11, peeled and cut into 8 strips	1

■ Combine the cooked rice with the chives and the first egg. Spread and pack the rice mixture evenly over the bottom and up the sides of a lightly sprayed deep 10 inch (25 cm) pie plate. Press with a rubber spatula to ensure there are no holes. Bake the rice shell in a 350°F (175°C) oven for 5 minutes. ■ Combine the next 9 ingredients in a large bowl. Mix well. Gently pour into the rice shell. Arrange the red pepper strips in a pinwheel over the top. ■ Bake, uncovered, in a 350°F (175°C) oven for 45 minutes or until the center is set. Immediately run a knife around the edge to loosen the crust. Let stand 10 minutes before cutting.

One wedge… Energy 245cal/1025kJ;
Fat 8.8g; Protein 18g; Carbohydrates 23g

Tamale Pie

Make and bake in 1 hour. Just add a salad to complete this meal. Serves 6.

1½ lbs.	Lean ground beef	680 g
2	Garlic cloves, minced	2
28 oz.	Canned stewed tomatoes, with juice, chopped	796 mL
2 tsp.	Chili powder	10 mL
⅛ tsp.	Salt	0.5 mL
⅛ tsp.	Freshly ground pepper	0.5 mL
¼ cup	Chopped fresh parsley	60 mL

TOPPING

1 cup	All-purpose flour	250 mL
¾ cup	Cornmeal	175 mL
1 tbsp.	Granulated sugar	15 mL
2 tsp.	Baking powder	10 mL
½ tsp.	Baking soda	2 mL
½ tsp.	Salt	2 mL
3 tbsp.	Grated Parmesan cheese	50 mL
1	Large egg	1
1 cup	1% buttermilk or sour milk (see Note)	250 mL
¼ cup	Vegetable oil	60 mL
3 dashes	Hot pepper sauce	3 dashes

■ Scramble-fry the beef and garlic in a large non-stick skillet until the beef is browned. Drain. Add the tomatoes and chili powder. Bring to a boil. Reduce the heat and simmer until the mixture is the consistency of a thick spaghetti sauce. Add the salt, pepper and parsley. Transfer to an ungreased deep 10 inch (25 cm) pie plate.
■ Stir the flour, cornmeal, sugar, baking powder, baking soda and salt together in a large bowl. Mix well. Add the Parmesan cheese and toss lightly. ■ Beat the egg, buttermilk, oil and hot pepper sauce together well in a separate bowl. Add the egg mixture to the dry ingredients. Stir until the dry ingredients are just moistened. Spread the cornmeal mixture evenly over the meat mixture. ■ Bake in a 375°F (190°C) oven for 30 minutes or until the topping is golden and a wooden toothpick inserted in the center comes out clean.

Note: To make sour milk, add milk to 1 tbsp. (15 mL) white vinegar in a measuring cup. Stir.

One serving… Energy 486cal/2033kJ; Fat 22g; Protein 29g; Carbohydrate 44g

Spaghetti Pie

From start to finish in less than 45 minutes.
Cuts into 6 wedges.

8 oz.	Spaghetti pasta, uncooked	250 g
1 tsp.	Dried sweet basil, crumbled	5 mL
1 lb.	Lean ground beef	454 g
14 oz.	Tomato sauce	398 mL
1	Garlic clove, minced	1
1 tsp.	Dried oregano	5 mL
¼ cup	Chopped sun-dried tomatoes, softened in boiling water for 5 minutes before chopping	60 mL
6 oz.	Jar marinated artichoke hearts, drained and rinsed	170 g
1 cup	Grated part skim mozzarella cheese	250 mL

■ Cook the pasta according to package directions. Drain well. ■ Toss the pasta with the basil and press firmly against the bottom and sides of a lightly sprayed 2½ quart (2.5 L) casserole dish or a deep 10 inch (25 cm) pie plate to form a thick "crust". ■ Scramble-fry the beef in a non-stick skillet. Drain. Add the tomato sauce, garlic, oregano and sun-dried tomatoes. Cover and simmer for 6 minutes, stirring occasionally. Pour the hot mixture into the spaghetti crust. ■ Arrange the artichoke hearts in the sauce mixture. Bake, uncovered, in a 350°F (175°C) oven for 15 to 20 minutes. ■ Sprinkle with the cheese. Bake for 5 minutes or until the cheese is melted.

One wedge… Energy 362cal/1513kJ;
Fat 10.4g; Protein 26g; Carbohydrate 41g

Cabbage Roll Casserole

Ready in under 2 hours. Easy to prepare.
Serves 6.

1 lb.	Lean ground beef	454 g
1	Large onion, chopped	1
1	Garlic clove, minced	1
1 tbsp.	Worcestershire sauce	15 mL
1 tsp.	Salt	5 mL
¼ tsp.	Freshly ground pepper	1 mL
14 oz.	Canned crushed tomatoes	398 mL
1¼ cups	Water	300 mL
½ cup	Long grain white rice, uncooked	125 mL
3 cups	Coarsely shredded cabbage	750 mL
¼ cup	Grated medium Cheddar cheese	60 mL

■ Scramble-fry the beef with the onion, garlic, Worcestershire sauce, salt and pepper until the beef is browned. Drain. ■ Stir in the tomato, water and rice. Simmer for 5 minutes. Place 2 cups (500 mL) of the cabbage in a lightly sprayed 3 quart (3 L) casserole dish. Spoon the beef mixture over top. Sprinkle with the remaining 1 cup (250 mL) of cabbage. ■ Cover and bake in a 325°F (160°C) oven for 1½ hours. Remove the lid and sprinkle with the cheese. Bake for 5 minutes or until the cheese is melted.

One serving… Energy 228cal/956kJ;
Fat 8.3g; Protein 18g; Carbohydrate 21g

Creamy Greek Bake

Simple, quicker version of the traditional Greek pastitsio casserole. Serves 6.

½ cup	Low-fat salad dressing (or mayonnaise)	125 mL
¼ cup	All-purpose flour	60 mL
2 cups	1% milk	500 mL
½ tsp.	Salt	2 mL
1 lb.	Lean ground beef	454 g
1 cup	Chopped onion	250 mL
1	Garlic clove, minced	1
5½ oz.	Tomato paste	156 mL
¼ tsp.	Ground cinnamon	1 mL
1	Large egg, fork-beaten	1
¼ tsp.	Ground nutmeg	1 mL
½ cup	Grated Parmesan cheese	125 mL
1½ cups	Elbow macaroni, cooked and drained	375 mL
	Paprika	

■ Whisk together the salad dressing and flour until smooth. Gradually whisk in the milk. Add the salt and simmer, stirring frequently, until thickened. Remove from the heat and pour into a medium bowl. Let the white sauce cool while preparing the meat sauce. ■ Scramble-fry the beef in a non-stick skillet with the onion and garlic until the beef is browned and the onion is soft. Drain. Stir in the tomato paste and cinnamon. Remove from the heat. ■ Stir the beaten egg, nutmeg and cheese into the white sauce. Mix well. Stir in the macaroni. In a lightly sprayed 3 quart (3 L) casserole dish, layer the macaroni mixture in three parts alternately with the beef mixture in two parts, beginning and ending with the macaroni mixture. Sprinkle with paprika. ■ Bake, covered, in a 350°F (175°) oven for 20 to 25 minutes or until hot and set.

One serving… Energy 371cal/1551kJ;
Fat 16.6g; Protein 25g; Carbohydrate 30g

Fast Fixin' Nacho Casserole

Quick way to use leftover beef. Only 5 minutes to prepare. Serves 4.

1¼ cups	Coarsely chopped cooked lean beef	300 mL
¾ cup	Salsa (mild, medium or hot)	175 mL
⅓ cup	Grated Monterey Jack cheese	75 mL
⅔ cup	Grated Monterey Jack cheese	150 mL
	Corn tortilla chips	

■ Combine the beef, salsa and first amount of cheese in a medium bowl. Turn into a lightly sprayed 1 quart (1 L) casserole dish. Cover and bake in a 350°F (175°C) oven for 20 minutes.

■ Top with the second amount of cheese. Bake, uncovered, in a 350°F (175°C) oven for 10 minutes or until the cheese is melted. Surround individual servings with chips.

One serving… Energy 269cal/1126kJ;
Fat 14.8g; Protein 21g; Carbohydrate 13g

Jambalaya Casserole

Preparation time only 15 minutes. A good make-ahead. Serves 6.

1 lb.	Lean ground beef	454 g
1	Garlic clove, minced	1
1	Medium onion, chopped	1
1	Green pepper, chopped	1
1 tbsp.	Chopped fresh parsley	15 mL
½ tsp.	Worcestershire sauce	2 mL
½ tsp.	Chili powder	2 mL
1 tsp.	Salt	5 mL
¼ tsp.	Pepper	1 mL
28 oz.	Canned stewed tomatoes, with juice, chopped	796 mL
¾ cup	Long grain white rice, uncooked	175 mL
1	Bay leaf	1
1 tsp.	Paprika	5 mL

■ Scramble-fry the beef with the garlic and onion until the beef is no longer pink. Drain. Combine the remaining ingredients in a large bowl. Add the beef mixture. Stir well. Place in a lightly sprayed 3 quart (3 L) casserole dish.

■ Bake, covered, in a 350°F (175°C) oven for 1¼ hours or until the rice is cooked.

One serving… Energy 249cal/1040kJ; Fat 6.8g; Protein 17g; Carbohydrate 31g

Easy One-Dish Dinner

Begin at least 2 hours ahead. Preparation time only 20 minutes. Serves 6.

½	Medium onion, sliced	½
½ cup	Long grain white rice, uncooked	125 mL
4	Medium carrots, thinly sliced	4
3	Medium potatoes, thinly sliced	3
12 oz.	Canned kernel corn, drained	341 mL
½ tsp.	Salt	2 mL
¼ tsp.	Pepper	1 mL
1 lb.	Lean ground beef	454 g
½ tsp.	Salt	2 mL
¼ tsp.	Pepper	1 mL
¼ cup	Diced green pepper	60 mL
½ cup	Diced celery	125 mL
1¾ cups	Vegetable juice (such as V8)	425 mL

■ Layer the first 5 ingredients in the order listed above in a lightly sprayed 3 quart (3 L) casserole dish. Sprinkle with the first amounts of salt and pepper. Crumble the uncooked beef over the top. Pat down gently. Sprinkle with the second amounts of salt and pepper. Layer the green pepper and celery. Pour the juice over.

■ Cover and bake in a 350°F (175°C) oven for 2 hours or until the carrot and potato are tender.

One serving… Energy 351cal/1467kJ; Fat 12g; Protein 19g; Carbohydrate 43g

CHAPTER 5

Entrées

Stuffed Manicotti, page 78

Swiss Steak and Peppers

Remove the seeds and ribs from jalapeño peppers for a milder flavor. Serves 6.

1 tsp.	Vegetable oil	5 mL
1½ lbs.	Minute steaks, cut into serving size pieces	680 g
½ tsp.	Dried thyme	2 mL
¾ tsp.	Salt	4 mL
¼ tsp.	Pepper	1 mL
1	Medium onion, chopped	1
1	Jalapeño pepper, with seeds and ribs, cut into ⅛ inch (3 mm) slices (wear gloves)	1
¼ cup	Water	60 mL
4	Medium tomatoes, chopped	4
½	Green pepper, cut into 1 inch (2.5 cm) chunks	½
½	Yellow pepper, cut into 1 inch (2.5 cm) chunks	½

■ Heat the oil in a large non-stick skillet until hot. Place the steaks in the skillet and brown on both sides. Season with the thyme, salt and pepper. Top with the onion and jalapeño pepper. ■ Add the water. Cover tightly and simmer for 45 minutes. ■ Add the tomato and peppers. Cover and continue to simmer for 30 minutes. Remove the beef and vegetables to a warmed platter. ■ Cook the sauce, uncovered, for 8 to 10 minutes or until reduced and slightly thickened, stirring frequently. ■ Return the beef and vegetables to the sauce mixture to heat through.

One serving… Energy 169cal/706kJ;
Fat 5.2g; Protein 23g; Carbohydrates 7g

Penne with Wine Vegetable Sauce

Lots of chopping but ready in 40 minutes. Serves 6.

2 tbsp.	Hard margarine	30 mL
3 tbsp.	All-purpose flour	50 mL
1 cup	Skim evaporated milk	250 mL
1 lb.	Lean ground beef	454 g
1	Large onion, cut in lengthwise slivers	1
4	Garlic cloves, minced	4
3 cups	Sliced fresh mushrooms	750 mL
1	Medium red pepper, cut in 2 inch (5 cm) strips	1
1 cup	Dry white wine	250 mL
28 oz.	Canned tomatoes, with juice, chopped	796 mL
¼ cup	Finely chopped fresh sweet basil	60 mL
8 oz.	Penne pasta, uncooked	250 g

GARNISH

Freshly ground pepper
Grated Parmesan cheese

■ Melt the margarine in a small saucepan. Stir in the flour. Gradually whisk in the milk until the sauce is smooth and bubbling. Remove from the heat. Cover and set aside. ■ Scramble-fry the beef in a large saucepan until the beef is no longer pink. Drain. Add the onion and garlic and sauté until the onion is soft. Add the mushrooms and red pepper and cook for 5 minutes or until the vegetables release their juices and the mixture is bubbling. ■ Add the wine and tomato and bring the mixture to a boil again. Stir in the white sauce and basil. Keep warm over low heat. ■ Cook the pasta according to package directions. Drain and combine with the meat sauce. ■ Sprinkle with pepper and Parmesan cheese.

One serving… Energy 435cal/1818kJ;
Fat 11.5g; Protein 25g; Carbohydrate 51g

Spaghetti Meat Sauce

Serve this over hot spaghetti with grated Parmesan cheese. Serves 6.

1 lb.	Lean ground beef	454 g
2	Medium onions, chopped	2
2	Large celery stalks, chopped	2
1	Medium green pepper, chopped	1
1	Garlic clove, minced	1
14 oz.	Canned crushed tomatoes	398 mL
28 oz.	Canned tomatoes, with juice, chopped	796 mL
⅓ cup	Water	75 mL
3 tbsp.	Chopped fresh parsley	50 mL
1 tsp.	Dried oregano	5 mL
1	Bay leaf	1
1 tbsp.	Chopped fresh sweet basil	15 mL
½ tsp.	Salt	2 mL
½ tsp.	Granulated sugar	2 mL
1 tsp.	Crushed chilies	5 mL
	Freshly ground pepper, to taste	

GARNISH

Grated Parmesan cheese

■ Scramble-fry the beef with the onion, celery, green pepper and garlic in a large saucepan until the beef is no longer pink. Drain. ■ Stir in the remaining ingredients and bring the sauce to a boil. Reduce the heat. Simmer, uncovered, for 45 minutes or until the vegetables are soft and the sauce is thickened. Discard the bay leaf.

One serving… Energy 181cal/758kJ; Fat 7g; Protein 16g; Carbohydrate 15g

Stuffed Manicotti

Assemble in the morning. Bake in the afternoon. Makes 14 stuffed manicotti plus 5 cups (1.25 L) sauce.

1 lb.	Lean ground beef	454 g
2 tsp.	Dried oregano	10 mL
1 tsp.	Granulated sugar	5 mL
14 oz.	Tomato sauce	398 mL
28 oz.	Canned stewed tomatoes, with juice, chopped	796 mL
2 cups	Part skim ricotta cheese	500 mL
⅓ cup	Grated Parmesan cheese	75 mL
¾ cup	Grated part skim mozzarella cheese	175 mL
2	Large eggs	2
2¼ cups	Chopped fresh spinach	560 mL
14	Manicotti pasta shells, uncooked	14
1 cup	Grated part skim mozzarella cheese	250 mL

■ Scramble-fry the beef in a medium saucepan. Drain. Stir in the oregano, sugar, tomato sauce and tomatoes. Simmer, covered, for 10 minutes while preparing the manicotti shells. ■ Combine the 3 cheeses with the eggs and spinach. Mix well. Stuff the uncooked manicotti shells with the cheese mixture. Spread 1 cup (250 mL) of the meat sauce in the bottom of an ungreased 9 x 13 inch (22 x 33 cm) baking pan. Arrange the 14 stuffed pasta shells in a single layer on top. Pour the remaining sauce over the manicotti. Cover tightly with foil. Bake in a 350°F (175°C) oven for 1¼ hours. ■ Sprinkle with the second amount of mozzarella cheese and continue to bake, uncovered, 5 to 8 minutes or until the cheese is melted.

One manicotti plus 1/3 cup (75 mL) sauce… Energy 222cal/929kJ; Fat 9.5g; Protein 18g; Carbohydrate 17g

Pasta Italia

Allow 1½ hours to prepare and cook. Serves 6.

1 lb.	Sirloin steak, cut into ¾ inch (2 cm) cubes	454 g
3	Garlic cloves, minced	3
1 tsp.	Olive oil	5 mL
14 oz.	Canned crushed tomatoes	398 mL
¾ cup	Water	175 mL
1	Medium red pepper, diced	1
1	Medium yellow pepper, diced	1
1	Medium zucchini, with peel, diced	1
1 tsp.	Olive oil	5 mL
¼ tsp.	Crushed chilies	1 mL
2 tbsp.	Chopped fresh sweet basil	30 mL
¾ tsp.	Dried oregano	4 mL
½ tsp.	Salt	2 mL
18	Whole pitted ripe olives	18
14 oz.	Canned artichoke hearts, drained and quartered	398 mL
8 oz.	Fusilli pasta, uncooked	250 g

■ Cook the beef cubes and garlic in the first amount of oil in a non-stick skillet or wok for 3 to 5 minutes. Add the tomato and water. Cover and simmer for 45 minutes to 1 hour.

■ Stir-fry the peppers and zucchini in the second amount of oil in a separate non-stick skillet or wok until the juices are released. Add the chilies, basil, oregano and salt and simmer for 5 minutes. Pour over the beef mixture and add the olives and artichokes. Mix well and keep warm.

■ Prepare the pasta according to package directions. Drain. Serve the beef and vegetables over the pasta.

One serving… Energy 317cal/1327kJ;
Fat 6.2g; Protein 23g; Carbohydrates 43g

Goulash with Roasted Pepper

Substitute regular paprika for the Hungarian. Flavor will be slightly less pungent. Spoon into center of broad noodles or rice. Serves 4.

1 lb.	Inside round steak, cut across the grain into thin strips	454 g
1 tsp.	Olive oil	5 mL
1	Medium onion, cut into lengthwise slivers	1
1	Large garlic clove, minced	1
1½ tbsp.	Hungarian paprika	25 mL
6	Large plum tomatoes, sliced	6
10 oz.	Condensed beef consommé	284 mL
4	Green, red or yellow Roasted Peppers, page 11, peeled and cut into strips	4
½ tsp.	Salt	2 mL
	Freshly ground pepper, to taste	
2 tbsp.	All-purpose flour	30 mL
⅔ cup	Non-fat sour cream	150 mL

■ Brown the beef in the oil in a Dutch oven. Add the onion, garlic and paprika. Stir and cook for 8 to 10 minutes or until the onion is soft. Add the tomato slices and consommé. Cover and simmer for 1 hour or until the beef is tender. ■ Stir in the roasted pepper strips and salt. Season with pepper and simmer, uncovered, for 10 to 15 minutes. Stir the flour into the sour cream and slowly add to the beef mixture. Continue to stir until thickened.

One serving… Energy 266cal/1108kJ; Fat 6.5g; Protein 30g; Carbohydrate 24g

Pineapple Meatloaf

Prepare the pineapple sauce while the meatloaf is baking. Cuts into 10 slices.

2 lbs.	Lean ground beef	900 g
2 cups	Fresh bread crumbs	500 mL
⅔ cup	Barbecue sauce	150 mL
2	Large eggs	2
1 tsp.	Salt	5 mL
	Pepper, to taste	
19 oz.	Canned sliced pineapple, juice reserved	540 mL

PINEAPPLE SAUCE

	Reserved pineapple juice	
1 tbsp.	Cornstarch	15 mL
½ cup	Barbecue sauce	125 mL

GARNISH

Whole green maraschino cherries

■ Combine the beef, bread crumbs and first amount of barbecue sauce. ■ Add the eggs, salt and pepper. Mix well. Firmly pack the beef mixture into a greased 9 x 5 x 3 inch (22 x 12 x 7 cm) loaf pan. Bake in a 350°F (175°C) oven for 1 hour. Drain. Invert the meatloaf onto an ovenproof platter. Cut the meatloaf into 10 slices, keeping the slices upright. Alternate the meatloaf slices with the pineapple slices. ■ Combine the pineapple juice with the cornstarch. Bring to a boil, stirring until thickened and clear. Add the second amount of barbecue sauce and heat. ■ Baste the meatloaf and pineapple slices with the pineapple sauce. Garnish the top with cherries using toothpicks. Return the meatloaf to the oven for 15 minutes. Serve with the remaining sauce.

One slice… Energy 238cal/995kJ;
Fat 9.4g; Protein 19g; Carbohydrate 18g

Oriental Stuffed Meatloaf

Best served the same day. Cuts into 8 slices.

1½ lbs.	Lean ground beef	680 g
½ cup	Chopped green onion	125 mL
1	Garlic clove, minced	1
2 tsp.	Freshly grated gingerroot	10 mL
1	Large egg	1
3 tbsp.	Black bean sauce or soy sauce	50 mL
3	Fresh bread slices, processed into crumbs	3

FILLING

8 oz.	Canned water chestnuts, drained and chopped	227 mL
2	Medium red Roasted Peppers, page 11, slivered	2

GLAZE

¼ cup	Black bean sauce	60 mL
¼ cup	Pineapple juice or water	60 mL
1 tsp.	Cornstarch	5 mL
1 tsp.	Brown sugar	5 mL

■ Combine the beef with the next 6 ingredients. Mix well.
■ Pat ½ of the beef mixture into a rectangular shape about 12 x 5 inch (30 x 12 cm) on a greased baking sheet. Sprinkle with the water chestnuts and lay the pepper slivers not quite to the edges of the beef. ■ Pat the remaining beef mixture into a rectangle 12 x 5 inch (30 x 12 cm) on waxed paper. Turn over onto the one on the baking sheet and remove the waxed paper. Seal the edges. Smooth the meatloaf to a rounded shape. Bake in a 350°F (175°C) oven for 45 minutes. ■ Combine the 4 glaze ingredients in a small saucepan. Simmer until slightly thickened. Brush generously over the meatloaf. Bake the meatloaf for 15 minutes to set the glaze.

One slice… Energy 204cal/854kJ; Fat 8.7g; Protein 18g; Carbohydrate 13g

Classic Meatloaf

Substitute a vegetable juice (such as V8) for a zestier taste. Cuts into 8 slices.

1½ lbs.	Lean ground beef	680 g
1 cup	Rolled oats (not instant)	250 mL
¼ cup	Finely chopped onion	60 mL
¼ cup	Finely chopped celery	60 mL
¼ cup	Finely chopped green pepper	60 mL
1½ tsp.	Salt	7 mL
¼ tsp.	Pepper	1 mL
¼ tsp.	Ground sage	1 mL
2	Large eggs, fork-beaten	2
⅔ cup	Tomato juice	150 mL

■ Combine all the ingredients in a large bowl. Mix very well. Pack firmly into an ungreased 9 x 5 x 3 inch (22 x 12 x 7 cm) loaf pan.
■ Bake in a 350°F (175°C) oven for 1¼ hours. Let stand for 10 minutes before cutting.

One slice… Energy 289cal/1209kJ; Fat 15.5g; Protein 21g; Carbohydrate 15g

Pesto Meatloaf Roll

Serve with Fresh Tomato Salsa, page 13 and a lightly buttered pasta. Cuts into 8 slices.

1½ lbs.	Lean ground beef	680 g
1 cup	Dry bread crumbs	250 mL
1	Large egg	1
1	Medium onion, finely chopped	1
2 tsp.	Beef bouillon powder	10 mL
½ cup	Chopped sun-dried tomatoes, softened in boiling water 5 minutes before chopping	125 mL
3 tbsp.	Tomato paste	50 mL
¼ cup	Water	60 mL

PESTO

1½ cups	Fresh sweet basil leaves, lightly packed	375 mL
6 tbsp.	Pine nuts	100 mL
3	Garlic cloves, crushed	3
6 tbsp.	Olive oil	100 mL
6 tbsp.	Grated Parmesan cheese	100 mL

■ Combine the beef with the next 7 ingredients. Spray a large piece of foil with no-stick cooking spray. Pat the beef into a 12 x 10 inch (30 x 25 cm) rectangle. ■ Combine the 5 pesto ingredients in a food processor. Process for 1 to 2 minutes. ■ Spread the pesto on the beef. Roll up from the longer edge, using the foil as a guide and pulling the foil back as you roll. Carefully place the roll, seam side down, onto an ungreased baking sheet. Bake in a 325°F (160°C) oven for 1 hour.

One slice… Energy 372cal/1556kJ; Fat 24.3g; Protein 23g; Carbohydrate 17g

Stir-Fry Stroganoff

Serve over hot broad noodles or rice. Serves 4.

1½ lbs.	Sirloin steak, cut into ¼ inch (6 mm) strips	680 g
1	Medium onion, sliced	1
2 cups	Thinly sliced fresh mushrooms	500 mL
2 tbsp + 1 tsp.	All-purpose flour	35 mL
½ tsp.	Dry mustard powder	2 mL
2 tbsp.	Tomato paste	30 mL
10 oz.	Condensed beef consommé	284 mL
1 tbsp.	Worcestershire sauce	15 mL
½ cup	Low-fat yogurt (or sour cream)	125 mL
¼ cup	Chopped fresh parsley	60 mL

■ Stir-fry the beef strips in a non-stick skillet or wok until no longer pink. Add the onion and mushrooms and sauté until the onion is soft. Remove the beef and vegetables from the skillet, leaving any liquid.
■ Combine the flour, mustard and tomato paste in a small bowl. Add the consommé and Worcestershire sauce. Mix well. Stir slowly into the liquid in the skillet. Cook and stir until thickened. Add the beef and vegetables. ■ Blend in the yogurt and parsley. Heat thoroughly being careful not to boil.

One serving… Energy 283cal/1182kJ;
Fat 6.7g; Protein 41g; Carbohydrate 13g

Rolled Steak Florentine

An inexpensive company dish. Allow 2½ hours to assemble and bake. Makes 8 steak rolls.

2¼ lbs.	Flank or round steak	1 kg
10 oz.	Fresh or frozen spinach, cooked, squeezed dry and chopped	300 g
¾ cup	Fresh bread crumbs	175 mL
½ cup	Grated medium Cheddar cheese	125 mL
1	Large egg, fork-beaten	1
½ tsp.	Poultry seasoning	2 mL
¼ tsp.	Salt	1 mL
	Pepper, to taste	
7½ oz.	Tomato sauce	213 mL
1 tsp.	Beef bouillon powder	5 mL
½ cup	Boiling water	125 mL
1	Small garlic clove, minced	1
2 tbsp.	All-purpose flour	30 mL
¼ cup	Cold water	60 mL

■ Cut the steak into 8, 3 x 4 inch (7.5 x 10 cm) pieces. Pound to ¼ inch (6 mm) thickness. ■ Combine the cooked spinach with the next 6 ingredients and mix well. Divide among the flattened steaks and spread evenly over the surface of each. ■ Roll up, starting with the narrow edge. Secure with metal skewers or string. ■ Broil the steak rolls 4 inches (10 cm) from the heat, turning until nicely browned. Combine the tomato sauce, bouillon powder, water and garlic and pour over the steak rolls in an ungreased 3 quart (3 L) casserole dish. Cover and bake in a 350°F (175°C) oven for 1½ hours or until tender, turning the rolls after 1 hour. Remove the rolls to a warm platter.
■ Combine the flour and water in a small cup until smooth. Stir slowly into the liquid left in the casserole dish. Heat until thickened. Serve with the steak rolls.

One roll… Energy 279cal/1168kJ;
Fat 12.5g; Protein 33g; Carbohydrate 8g

Greek Pizza

Save time by using a pre-baked flatbread crust. Reduce baking time by 10 minutes. Cuts into 8 slices.

½ lb.	Lean ground beef	225 g
2	Garlic cloves, minced	2
1 cup	Coarsely chopped onion	250 mL
10 oz.	Frozen spinach, thawed, squeezed dry and chopped	300 g
1 tsp.	Dried sweet basil	5 mL
½ tsp.	Lemon pepper	2 mL
½ cup	Chopped sun-dried tomatoes, softened in boiling water 5 minutes before chopping	125 mL
1	Homemade or bought unbaked pizza crust (12 inches, 30 cm)	1
1 tbsp.	Olive oil	15 mL
4 oz.	Crumbled feta cheese	125 g
¼ cup	Grated Parmesan cheese	60 mL
¼ cup	Sliced pitted ripe olives	60 mL

■ Scramble-fry the beef, garlic and onion in a non-stick skillet until the beef is browned and the onion is soft. Drain. Remove from the heat and add the spinach, basil, lemon pepper and tomato. Toss lightly. Brush the pizza crust with the oil. Spread the beef mixture over the crust. Sprinkle with the cheeses and olives. Bake in a 425°F (220°C) oven for 20 minutes.

One slice… Energy 252cal/1056kJ;
Fat 9.8g; Protein 14g; Carbohydrate 28g

Easy Pizza

Easy to prepare. Easy to assemble.
Cuts into 8 slices.

2 cups	Biscuit mix	500 mL
½ cup	Warm water	125 mL
1 tbsp.	Olive oil	15 mL
¾ cup	Pizza sauce or spicy spaghetti sauce	175 mL
½ lb.	Lean ground beef, cooked and drained	225 g
½	Medium onion, chopped	½
1 tsp.	Dried oregano	5 mL
1 cup	Sliced fresh mushrooms	250 mL
1½ cups	Grated part skim mozzarella cheese	375 mL
1 cup	Chopped green pepper	250 mL

■ Combine the biscuit mix and water in a medium bowl. Mix well until the dough forms into a ball. Knead the dough on a floured surface, adding more mix as required to form a smooth ball that is no longer sticky. ■ Lightly grease a 12 inch (30 cm) pizza pan and the palms of your hands with the oil. Press the dough into the bottom and ½ inch (12 mm) up the sides of the pizza pan, using more oil as required. ■ Layer on the remaining ingredients in the order given. Bake in a 450°F (230°C) oven for 12 to 15 minutes or until the crust is browned and the cheese is melted. Place under the broiler for 3 to 4 minutes to brown the cheese, if desired.

One slice... Energy 323cal/1353kJ;
Fat 14.8g; Protein 18g; Carbohydrate 30g

Traditional Pizza

If using an unbaked pizza crust, add 10 minutes to the baking time. Cuts into 8 slices.

½ lb.	Lean ground beef	225 g
1 cup	Chopped onion	250 mL
2 cups	Sliced fresh mushrooms	500 mL
½ x 5½ oz.	Tomato paste	½ x 156 mL
1	Italian style flatbread (12 inches, 30 cm)	1
1 tsp.	Dried sweet basil	5 mL
½ tsp.	Dried oregano	2 mL
1½ cups	Grated part skim mozzarella cheese	375 mL
1 cup	Grated Asiago cheese	250 mL
1	Medium yellow pepper, cut into rings	1
1	Large tomato, seeded and diced	1

■ Scramble-fry the beef and onion in a non-stick skillet until the beef is browned. Drain. Add the mushrooms and continue cooking until the mushroom liquid is evaporated. Spread a thin layer of tomato paste over the flatbread and sprinkle with the basil and oregano. Layer the beef mixture over the sauce. Top with the cheeses. ■ Arrange the pepper rings over the top and sprinkle with the diced tomato. Bake in a 425°F (220°C) oven for 10 minutes or until hot and the cheese is melted. Place under the broiler for 3 to 4 minutes to brown the cheese, if desired.

One slice... Energy 319cal/1333kJ;
Fat 11.3g; Protein 21g; Carbohydrate 35g

Greek Pita Pizzas

Slice each pizza into 8 to 10 small wedges for appetizers. Makes 6 individual pizzas.

10 oz.	Frozen spinach	300 g
1 lb.	Lean ground beef	454 g
2	Garlic cloves, minced	2
½ cup	Finely chopped onion	125 mL
½ tsp.	Salt	2 mL
¼ tsp.	Freshly ground pepper	1 mL
½ tsp.	Dried oregano	2 mL
1 tbsp.	Finely chopped fresh sweet basil	15 mL
½ cup	Grated part skim mozzarella cheese	125 mL
½ cup	Crumbled feta cheese	125 mL
6	Pita breads (7 inch,17.5 cm size)	6
1-2	Medium tomatoes, seeded and diced	1-2
½ cup	Crumbled feta cheese	125 mL
½ cup	Sliced pitted ripe olives	125 mL

■ Cook the spinach according to package directions. Drain and squeeze dry. Chop into smaller pieces. Set aside. ■ Scramble-fry the beef, garlic and onion in a non-stick skillet until the beef is browned and the onion is soft. Drain. Stir in the chopped spinach and seasonings. Blend in the mozzarella cheese and the first amount of feta cheese. Remove from the heat. ■ Lay 3 of the pita breads on an ungreased 11 x 17 inch (28 x 43 cm) baking sheet and flatten as best you can. Spread ½ cup (125 mL) of the beef mixture on each pita. Sprinkle with diced tomato, feta cheese and olives. Place under a preheated broiler 4 to 6 inches (10 to 15 cm) from the heat. Broil for 6 minutes or until hot and starting to brown on the edges.

One pizza… Energy 505cal/2113kJ;
Fat 19.9g; Protein 32g; Carbohydrate 50g

Pizza Loaf

Use for a luncheon or for a teenage gathering.
Cuts into 16, 2 to 3 inch (5 to 7.5 cm) slices.

1½ lbs.	Lean ground beef	680 g
14 oz.	Spaghetti sauce	398 mL
1½ tsp.	Dried oregano	7 mL
1 cup	Chopped onion	250 mL
1	Medium red pepper, chopped	1
2 cups	Broccoli florets	500 mL
1	French bread loaf, cut in half horizontally	1
1½ cups	Grated part skim mozzarella cheese	375 mL
1½ cups	Grated medium Cheddar cheese	375 mL

■ Scramble-fry the beef in a non-stick skillet until no pink remains. Drain. Combine the beef, spaghetti sauce and oregano in a medium bowl. Set aside. ■ In the same skillet, stir-fry the vegetables until tender-crisp. ■ Place the loaf halves on an ungreased baking sheet. Spread the beef mixture over each half. Sprinkle ½ of the cheeses over the beef. ■ Top with the vegetables and the remaining cheeses. Bake in a 425°F (220°C) oven for 15 to 20 minutes or until the cheese is melted.

One slice… Energy 259cal/1081kJ;
Fat 11.3g; Protein 17g; Carbohydrate 23g

Oriental Tortilla Rolls

Quick way to use leftover roast beef or steak. Makes 8 rolls.

½ tsp.	Granulated sugar	2 mL
2 tsp.	Cornstarch	10 mL
1 tsp.	Freshly grated gingerroot	5 mL
1	Garlic clove, minced	1
1 tbsp.	Soy sauce	15 mL
1 tsp.	Beef bouillon powder	5 mL
½ cup	Boiling water	125 mL
8 oz.	Cooked lean beef, cut into thin strips	250 g
2 tsp.	Vegetable oil	10 mL
2	Large eggs, fork-beaten	2
1 tsp.	Vegetable oil	5 mL
2	Medium carrots, cut julienne	2
14 oz.	Canned whole baby corn, drained	398 mL
4	Green onions, sliced	4
2 cups	Fresh bean sprouts	500 mL
8	Flour tortillas (10 inch, 25 cm)	8
3 tbsp.	Plum sauce	50 mL

■ Combine the first 7 ingredients in a medium bowl and toss together with the beef. Set aside.
■ Heat the first amount of oil in a non-stick skillet or wok. Pour in the eggs. Cook for 2 minutes and then turn over for 1 minute more. Slide the egg out onto a cutting board and cut into long, fine slivers. Set aside. ■ Heat the next amount of oil in the skillet. Stir-fry the carrot for 2 minutes. Add the corn and onion and stir-fry 1 to 2 minutes. Make a well in the center of the vegetables and pour in the stirred beef and broth mixture. Stir and cook with the vegetables for 1 to 2 minutes or until bubbling and thickened. Add the bean sprouts and egg. Stir gently to heat through. Do not overcook. ■ Spread about 1 tsp. (5 mL) of the plum sauce down the center of each tortilla. Place 1 cup (250 mL) of filling on top of the plum sauce and fold the bottom of the tortilla up, and the sides in, envelope style.

One roll plus 1 cup (250 mL) filling... Energy 266cal/1115kJ; Fat 5.2g; Protein 17g; Carbohydrate 39g

Exotic Stuffed Peppers

Loaded with fiber and vitamins. Makes 8 stuffed pepper halves.

4	Medium yellow or red peppers	4

STUFFING

½ cup	Bulgur	125 mL
¾ cup	Boiling water	175 mL
½ lb.	Lean ground beef	225 g
5	Garlic cloves, minced	5
¼ cup	Chopped green onion	60 mL
¼ cup	Chopped celery	60 mL
¼ cup	Grated carrot	60 mL
3	Large plum tomatoes, diced	3
1 tbsp.	Finely chopped fresh parsley	15 mL
	Freshly ground pepper, to taste	
½ cup	Grated medium Cheddar cheese	125 mL
1 cup	Condensed beef broth	250 mL

■ Cut the peppers in half lengthwise through the stems. Remove the seeds and white ribs from insides. Set aside. ■ Combine the bulgur and boiling water. Let stand for 8 to 10 minutes or until the water is absorbed. ■ Scramble-fry the beef in a non-stick skillet until no longer pink. Drain. ■ Add the garlic, onion, celery, carrot and tomato and sauté for 5 minutes. Remove from the heat. Combine the soaked bulgur and beef mixture in a medium bowl. Add the parsley, pepper and cheese. Toss. ■ Drizzle ⅓ of the beef broth over the mixture to moisten. ■ Pack the ½ pepper shells with the mixture. Lay them in an ungreased 9 x 13 inch (22 x 33 cm) baking pan. Pour the remaining ⅔ of beef broth over the peppers and into the pan. Cover tightly with foil. Bake in a 375˚F (190˚C) oven for 30 to 40 minutes or until the peppers are tender-crisp.

One stuffed pepper half… Energy 138cal/578kJ; Fat 5.2g; Protein 10g; Carbohydrate 14g

Baked Meatballs In Wine

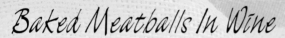

Make the day before. Cover and refrigerate after pouring sauce over meatballs. Remove from refrigerator 30 minutes before baking. Follow baking time in recipe. Serves 8.

MEATBALLS

2	Large eggs, fork-beaten	2
¾ cup	Fresh bread crumbs	175 mL
⅓ cup	1% milk	75 mL
¼ tsp.	Ground allspice	1 mL
1 tsp.	Salt	5 mL
⅛ tsp.	Pepper	0.5 mL
¼ cup	Finely minced onion	60 mL
2 lbs.	Lean ground beef	900 g

SAUCE

1	Small onion, minced	1
1 cup	Sliced fresh mushrooms	250 mL
2	Garlic cloves, minced	2
2 tbsp.	Hard margarine	30 mL
2 tbsp.	All-purpose flour	30 mL
10 oz.	Condensed beef consommé	284 mL
¼ cup	Dry red wine	60 mL

GARNISH

Chopped fresh parsley

■ Combine the 8 meatball ingredients in a large bowl. Mix well. ■ With partially wet hands, shape the beef mixture into 48 balls the size of golf balls. ■ Arrange the meatballs in a single layer on a large ungreased baking sheet. Bake in a 500°F (260°C) oven for 10 to 12 minutes or until browned. ■ Sauté the onion, mushrooms and garlic in the margarine for 5 minutes or until the liquid is evaporated and the onion is golden. Sprinkle with the flour. Mix well. Slowly add the consommé and wine. Cook until the sauce is thickened. ■ Place the meatballs in an ungreased 3 quart (3 L) casserole dish. Pour the sauce over the meatballs. Bake, covered, in a 350°F (175°C) oven for 30 minutes. ■ Garnish with parsley.

One serving (6 meatballs)…Energy 261cal/1091kJ; Fat 13.9g; Protein 25g; Carbohydrate 7g

Dijon Meatballs

Ample sauce to serve over pasta. Makes 24 meatballs with 2¼ cups (560 mL) sauce. Serves 4.

MEATBALLS

1 lb.	Lean ground beef	454 g
½ cup	Fresh bread crumbs	125 mL
¼ cup	Finely minced onion	60 mL
1 tbsp.	Dijon mustard	15 mL
½ tsp.	Salt	2 mL
¼ tsp.	Pepper	1 mL

SAUCE

3 tbsp.	All-purpose flour	50 mL
1 tbsp.	Cornstarch	15 mL
1½ tsp.	Beef bouillon powder	7 mL
1 cup	Water	250 mL
1 tsp.	Lemon juice	5 mL
1 cup	1% milk	250 mL
3 tbsp.	Finely chopped fresh chives	50 mL
2 tbsp.	Dijon mustard	30 mL
¼ tsp.	Freshly ground pepper	1 mL

■ Combine the 6 meatball ingredients in a large bowl. Mix well. Shape into 24 balls. Place on an ungreased baking sheet. Bake, uncovered, in a 400°F (205°C) oven for 20 minutes. ■ Mix the flour, cornstarch, bouillon powder, water and lemon juice in a large saucepan. Stir in the remaining ingredients. Cook, stirring constantly, until the mixture boils and thickens. Continue to boil for 1 minute. Add the meatballs and heat for 1 minute.

One serving (6 meatballs)… Energy 264cal/1104kJ; Fat 11.3g; Protein 25g; Carbohydrate 15g

Honey Garlic Meatballs

Shape into 68, 1 inch (2.5 cm) balls to use as a hot appetizer. Serve the sauce as a dip. Serves 8 as an entrée.

MEATBALLS

2 lbs.	Lean ground beef	900 g
4	Fresh bread slices, processed into crumbs	4
2	Large eggs	2
1 tsp.	Salt	5 mL
¼ tsp.	Cayenne pepper	1 mL

SAUCE

1 tbsp.	Hard margarine	15 mL
8	Garlic cloves, minced	8
14 oz.	Canned stewed tomatoes, with juice, puréed	398 mL
¾ cup	Liquid honey	175 mL
2 tsp.	Cornstarch	10 mL
¼ cup	Soy sauce	60 mL

■ Combine the 5 meatball ingredients in a large bowl. Mix well. Form into 48, 1½ inch (3.8 cm) balls. ■ Bake on an ungreased baking sheet in a 500°F (260°C) oven for 10 to 12 minutes. Remove the meatballs to an ungreased 2 quart (2 L) casserole dish. ■ Melt the margarine in a medium saucepan. Sauté the garlic until soft but not browned. Add the tomato and honey. Mix the cornstarch with the soy sauce and stir into the tomato mixture. Bring to a boil. Reduce the heat. Simmer, uncovered, for 10 minutes, stirring frequently. Pour the thickened sauce over the meatballs. ■ Bake, uncovered, in a 350°F (175°C) oven for 20 minutes or until the meatballs are glazed.

One serving (6 meatballs)… Energy 354cal/1482kJ; Fat 12.6g; Protein 24g; Carbohydrate 37g

Sesame Kabobs with Spinach

Soak 8, 10 inch (25 cm) bamboo skewers in water for 10 minutes while preparing the kabobs. Makes 8 kabobs with 2 cups (500 mL) cooked spinach.

⅓ cup	Soy sauce	75 mL
⅓ cup	Sesame oil	75 mL
2 tbsp.	Sesame seeds	30 mL
2 tbsp.	Freshly grated gingerroot	30 mL
1 lb.	Top, inside round or sirloin tip steak, cut into 1 inch (2.5 cm) cubes	454 g
1	Large red onion, cut into 8 wedges	1
1	Large yellow pepper, cut into 1 inch (2.5 cm) chunks	1
10 oz.	Fresh spinach, rinsed and drained	300 g
1	Large tomato, cut into wedges	1
	Reserved marinade	

■ Combine the first 4 ingredients in a medium bowl. Reserve ¼ cup (60 mL) of the marinade for the spinach. ■ Add the beef cubes to the remaining marinade. Cover and chill for 2 hours. ■ Thread the beef cubes onto the presoaked skewers alternately with the onion wedges and pepper chunks. Baste well with the marinade. Place the skewers on a broiler pan rack. Discard the first marinade. ■ Combine the spinach, tomato wedges and reserved marinade in the bottom of the broiler pan. Place the rack of skewers on top of the pan. Broil 7 to 9 inches (17.5 to 22 cm) from the heat for 12 to 15 minutes for medium rare, turning once. Drain the spinach and tomatoes and place on a warmed platter. Lay the kabobs on the spinach and serve immediately.

One kabob plus 1/4 cup (60 mL) spinach… Energy 128cal/534kJ; Fat 6.3g; Protein 13g; Carbohydrate 5g

Spanish Omelet

Prepare the filling in 15 minutes. Each omelet takes 3 minutes. Makes 6 stuffed omelets.

1	Medium onion, chopped	1
1	Medium yellow pepper, chopped	1
1	Small zucchini, with peel, sliced	1
1 tbsp.	Finely chopped fresh parsley	15 mL
2	Medium tomatoes, seeded and chopped	2
¼ tsp.	Dried oregano	1 mL
¼ tsp.	Salt	1 mL
¼ tsp.	Freshly ground pepper	1 mL
¾ lb.	Cooked lean beef, cut into thin strips	340 g
12	Large eggs	12
6 tbsp.	1% milk	100 mL
6 tsp.	Hard margarine	30 mL

■ Sauté the first 8 ingredients in a non-stick skillet for 3 to 5 minutes. Stir in the beef strips. Beat 2 of the eggs and 1 tbsp. (15 mL) of the milk with a fork in a small bowl. Melt 1 tsp. (5 mL) of the margarine in a small nonstick skillet. Pour in the egg mixture. Cook, without stirring, until the omelet is almost set. Spoon ⅙ of the beef mixture on ½ of the omelet. Fold the uncovered half over the top and continue cooking until the egg is set. ■ Repeat for the remaining 5 omelets.

One omelet with filling… Energy 279cal/1168kJ;
Fat 16.4g; Protein 25g; Carbohydrate 7g

Company Rouladen

Remove the toothpicks or string before serving. Serves 8, one roll each.

8	Bacon slices, cooked almost crisp, drained	8
8 oz.	Jar marinated mushrooms, drained and chopped	250 mL
8	Rouladen steaks, ¼ inch (6 mm) thick (about 1½ lbs., 680 g total)	8
¼ cup	All-purpose flour	60 mL
1 tsp.	Seasoned salt	5 mL
¼ tsp.	Pepper	1 mL
¾ cup	Water	175 mL
10 oz.	Condensed beef consommé	284 mL
½ cup	Chopped onion	125 mL
1	Garlic clove, minced	1
1	Bay leaf	1
3 tbsp.	All-purpose flour	50 mL
¼ cup	Water	60 mL

■ Cut the bacon into ½ inch (12 mm) pieces. Combine the bacon and the mushrooms in a small bowl. Place equal amounts of the bacon-mushroom mixture on each of the 8 steaks. Roll up, tucking in the ends as you roll. Secure with toothpicks or string. ■ Combine the first amount of flour, seasoned salt and pepper in a small plastic bag. Coat all the rolls with the flour mixture and place on a lightly sprayed broiler pan. Discard excess flour. ■ Broil the steaks 4 inches (10 cm) from the heat for 3 to 4 minutes per side, turning to brown evenly. Place in an ungreased 2 quart (2 L) casserole dish.
■ Combine the water, consommé, onion, garlic and bay leaf. Pour over the beef rolls. Cover. Bake in a 350°F (175°C) oven for 1 hour. Combine the second amounts of flour and water in a small cup until smooth. Stir into the liquid in the casserole dish. Continue to bake for 15 minutes until the beef is tender. Discard the bay leaf.

One roll… Energy 184cal/770kJ; Fat 6.4g; Protein 22g; Carbohydrate 9g

Beef in Pastry

Fussy but fast. Prepare, assemble and bake in less than 45 minutes. Serves 4.

2 tsp.	Olive oil	10 mL
½ lb.	Fresh mushrooms, finely chopped	225 g
3 tbsp.	Dry red wine	50 mL
¼ cup	Finely chopped green onion	60 mL
¼ tsp.	Dried thyme	1 mL
¼ tsp.	Salt	1 mL
⅛ tsp.	Pepper	0.5 mL
4 x 4 oz.	Tenderloin steaks, 1 inch (2.5 cm) thick	4 x 125 g
	Salt, to taste	
	Pepper, to taste	
6	Phyllo pastry sheets	6

■ Heat the oil in a large non-stick skillet until hot. Add the mushrooms. Sauté until tender. Add the wine and cook for 2 minutes or until the liquid is evaporated. Stir in the onion, thyme and first amounts of salt and pepper. Remove the mixture from the skillet and cool thoroughly. ■ Using the same skillet, cook the steaks 1½ minutes per side. The steaks will only be partially cooked. Do not overcook. Season with salt and pepper. ■ Layer all the phyllo sheets on a flat surface, spraying each sheet thoroughly with no-stick cooking spray. Cut the stacked layer lengthwise in half and then crosswise in half to make 4 equal portions. ■ Divide the mushroom mixture among the 4 portions and spread slightly in the center to the diameter of each steak. ■ Place the steaks on the mushroom mixture. Bring all 4 corners of the phyllo together and pinch and twist tightly to close. Lightly spray each "packet" with no-stick cooking spray and place on a lightly sprayed baking sheet. Immediately place in a 425°F (220°C) oven for 9 to 10 minutes or until golden brown. Let stand for 5 minutes and then serve immediately.

One serving... Energy 318cal/1332kJ; Fat 17.1g; Protein 25g; Carbohydrate 13g

Gourmet Stuffed Steak

Blanch the carrots and onions in boiling water for 4 minutes. Plunge immediately into cold water. Serves 6.

1½ lbs.	Flank steak	680 g

MARINADE

½ cup	Red wine vinegar	125 mL
2 tbsp.	Infused herb oil or vegetable oil	30 mL
1	Garlic clove, minced	1

STUFFING

5 oz.	Fresh or frozen spinach, cooked, squeezed dry and chopped	140 g
2	Medium carrots, blanched and cut in half lengthwise	2
2	Small onions, blanched and sliced	2
2	Large eggs, hard-boiled and quartered	2
1	Medium red pepper, sliced	1
2 tbsp.	Chopped fresh parsley	30 mL
1 tsp.	Salt	5 mL
⅛ tsp.	Pepper	0.5 mL

GRAVY

2 tbsp.	Beef bouillon powder	30 mL
4 cups	Boiling water	1 L
¼ cup	All-purpose flour	60 mL
1 cup	Cold water	250 mL
⅛ tsp.	Freshly ground pepper	0.5 mL
¼ tsp.	Salt	1 mL

■ "Butterfly" the flank steak by splitting it in half horizontally to within ½ inch (12 mm) from the edge. Do not slice apart completely. Open the steak and pound with a meat mallet to ¼ inch (6 mm) thickness. ■ Place the steak in a shallow dish or sealable plastic bag. Combine the 3 marinade ingredients and pour over the steak. Turn to coat. Cover or seal. Marinate in the refrigerator for 6 hours or overnight. ■ Remove the steak, discarding the marinade. Layer the stuffing ingredients evenly, in the order given, over the open steak, leaving a 3 inch (7.5 cm) uncovered flap at one end. Carefully roll the steak, jelly roll fashion, ending with the exposed steak, folding it over the edges. Tie with string to secure. Broil the roll, 4 inches (10 cm) from the heat, for 4 minutes on each side, turning until evenly browned. Place in a medium roaster. ■ Combine the bouillon powder and water in a large bowl. Pour over the roll. Cover and bake in a 350°F (175°C) oven for 1½ hours, turning once so that the top does not dry out. Remove the steak roll and let stand for 10 minutes before slicing. ■ Measure 3 cups (750 mL) of the liquid left in the roaster. Discard the remaining liquid. Spoon off any fat from the measured amount. Return to the roaster. Stir the flour into the water in a small bowl. Slowly stir into the liquid. Heat until thickened. Add the second amounts of salt and pepper. Serve with the sliced roll.

One serving... Energy 268cal/1121kJ; Fat 10.7g; Protein 30g; Carbohydrate 12g

Potatoes Olé

Use 6 medium baking potatoes and 1 lb. (454 g) of cooked beef but same amount of sauce to increase to 6 servings. Serves 4.

4	Large baking potatoes	4
12 oz.	Cooked lean beef, thinly sliced (about 2 cups, 500 mL)	340 g
2	Small onions, chopped	2
2	Garlic cloves, minced	2
2 tbsp.	Infused oil with garlic	30 mL
2 tbsp.	All-purpose flour	30 mL
½ tsp.	Chili powder	2 mL
½ tsp.	Ground cumin	2 mL
⅛ tsp.	Salt	0.5 mL
⅛ tsp.	Pepper	0.5 mL
1 cup	1% milk	250 mL
¼ cup	Grated sharp Cheddar cheese	60 mL

■ Scrub the potatoes well and bake in a 400°F (205°C) oven for 1 hour or until tender. Keep warm. ■ While the potatoes are baking, cut the beef slices into ½ inch (12 mm) strips. Set aside. ■ Sauté the onion and garlic in the oil in a non-stick skillet until the onion is soft. Stir in the flour and seasonings. Slowly add the milk, stirring constantly, until bubbling and thickened. ■ Cut a lengthwise slit in each potato, not quite to the bottom, and open part way. Fill with the beef strips. Spoon the sauce over top and sprinkle with the grated cheese. Place on a baking sheet and reheat in a 350°F (175°C) oven until the cheese is melted.

One serving... Energy 493cal/2062kJ; Fat 14.3g; Protein 31g; Carbohydrate 59g

Pepper Steak

Allow about 1 hour to prepare and cook. Serve immediately so that peppers stay tender–crisp. Serves 4.

1 lb.	Sirloin steak, ½ inch (12 mm) thick	454 g
1 tbsp.	Paprika	15 mL
1 tbsp.	Vegetable oil	15 mL
2	Garlic cloves, minced	2
10 oz.	Condensed beef consommé	284 mL
1 cup	Sliced green onions, including tops	250 mL
1	Medium red pepper, cut into strips	1
1	Medium yellow pepper, cut into strips	1
2 tbsp.	Cornstarch	30 mL
⅓ cup	Water	75 mL
¼ cup	Soy sauce	60 mL
2	Large tomatoes, cut into 8 wedges each	2

■ Pound the steak to ¼ inch (6 mm) thickness. Cut the pounded steak into ¼ inch (6 mm) wide strips. Sprinkle with the paprika and let stand a few minutes. ■ Heat the oil in a non-stick skillet or wok until hot. Stir-fry the beef strips until browned. Add the garlic and sauté for 1 minute. Stir in the consommé. Cover and simmer for 30 minutes. Stir in the green onion and peppers. Cover and cook for 5 minutes.

■ Blend the cornstarch with the water and soy sauce in a small cup. Stir into the beef mixture and cook about 2 minutes until clear and thickened. Add the tomato wedges and stir gently to heat through.

One serving… Energy 247cal/1033kJ; Fat 8.2g; Protein 29g; Carbohydrate 15g

Sweet and Sour Short Ribs

Allow just over 2 hours to parboil and bake. Prepare and sauté vegetables while ribs are simmering. Serves 6.

3 lbs.	Short ribs, cut in half crosswise	1.4 kg
1 cup	Boiling water	250 mL
1 tsp.	Vegetable oil	5 mL
¼ cup	Finely chopped onion	60 mL
1	Small garlic clove, minced	1
¼ cup	Finely chopped celery	60 mL
½ cup	Finely chopped green pepper	125 mL
1 cup	Pineapple juice	250 mL
½ cup	Water	125 mL
2 tsp.	Beef bouillon powder	10 mL
¼ cup	Brown sugar, packed	60 mL
½ cup	White vinegar	125 mL
1½ tbsp.	Soy sauce	25 mL
1 tbsp.	Cornstarch	15 mL
¼ cup	Water	60 mL

■ Simmer the short ribs in the first amount of water in a large saucepan for about 1½ hours. ■ Heat the oil in a non-stick skillet and sauté the onion, garlic, celery and green pepper until soft. Add the next 6 ingredients. Simmer for 5 minutes. ■ Combine the cornstarch and the third amount of water and slowly pour into the simmering sweet and sour sauce. Continue to simmer for 5 minutes or until thickened. ■ Remove the ribs from the saucepan and lay in an ungreased shallow baking pan. Pour the sauce over. Cover with foil and cook at 350°F (175°C) for 20 minutes, turning ribs once. Remove the foil. Turn the ribs again and cook, uncovered, 15 to 20 minutes.

One serving... Energy 296cal/1239kJ; Fat 13g; Protein 24g; Carbohydrate 20g

Maple Short Ribs

Mix the corn syrup and maple flavoring together first and adjust the taste to suit. Serves 4.

3 lbs.	Short ribs, bone-in	1.4 kg
1	Medium onion, sliced	1
2	Celery stalks, with leaves, coarsely diced	2
10	Black peppercorns	10
1½ cups	Corn or cane syrup	375 mL
1 tsp.	Maple flavoring	5 mL
¼ cup	Cider vinegar	60 mL
3 tbsp.	Chili sauce	50 mL
1	Small onion, finely chopped	1
1 tsp.	Worcestershire sauce	5 mL
¾ tsp.	Dry mustard powder	4 mL
½ tsp.	Salt	2 mL
⅛ tsp.	Pepper	0.5 mL

■ Place the ribs, onion, celery and peppercorns in a Dutch oven. Cover with water and bring to a boil. Cover and simmer for 1½ hours or until the beef is tender. Remove the ribs, discarding the liquid and vegetables. ■ Arrange the ribs in a lightly sprayed shallow roaster. ■ Combine the remaining ingredients and spoon over the ribs, turning to coat all sides. ■ Bake, uncovered, in a 325°F (160°C) oven for 30 minutes, stirring occasionally.

One serving… Energy 513cal/2145kJ;
Fat 18.2g; Protein 35g; Carbohydrate 52g

Saucy Short Ribs

Prepare the vegetables while the ribs are baking. Allow 3 hours total time. Serves 6.

3 lbs.	Short ribs, bone-in	1.4 kg
½ cup	Water	125 mL
1	Large Spanish onion or cooking onion, sliced	1
2	Large green peppers, sliced	2
1 lb.	Fresh mushrooms, sliced	454 g
¼ cup	Chopped pimiento	60 mL
5½ oz.	Tomato paste	156 mL
2 tbsp.	All-purpose flour	30 mL
2 x 10 oz.	Condensed beef broth	2 x 284 mL
½ tsp.	Dried oregano	2 mL
¼ tsp.	Cayenne pepper	1 mL
2 tbsp.	Worcestershire sauce	30 mL
¼ tsp.	Salt	1 mL
⅛ tsp.	Pepper	0.5 mL

■ Cut the ribs in serving size pieces and place in a roaster. Add the water and cover with the lid. ■ Bake in a 350°F (175°C) oven for 2 hours. Drain. ■ Cover the ribs with the vegetables. Combine the 8 remaining ingredients. Mix well and pour over the ribs. Cover and return to the oven for 1 hour, stirring occasionally, or until the meat pulls away from the bones.

One serving… Energy 303cal/1267kJ;
Fat 12.8g; Protein 31g; Carbohydrate 17g

CHAPTER 6

Roasts

Tangy Beef Roast, page 109

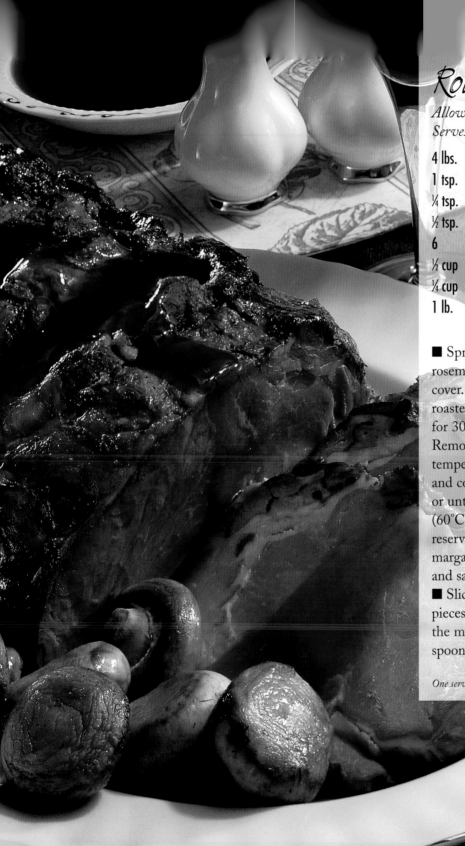

Royal Rib-Eye

Allow 30 minutes to prepare and about 1 hour to roast.
Serves 12.

4 lbs.	Boneless rib-eye roast	1.8 kg
1 tsp.	Salt	5 mL
¼ tsp.	Freshly ground pepper	1 mL
½ tsp.	Dried rosemary, crushed	2 mL
6	Bacon slices, cut in half	6
½ cup	Medium dry red wine	125 mL
¼ cup	Hard margarine	60 mL
1 lb.	Large fresh mushrooms	454 g
	(or 8 slices portobello mushrooms)	

■ Sprinkle the roast with the salt, pepper and rosemary. Lay the bacon slices over the top to form a cover. Place the roast in the bottom of a shallow roaster. ■ Roast, uncovered, in a 450°F (230°C) oven for 30 minutes. Remove the roast from the oven. Remove and discard the string and bacon. Reduce the temperature to 300°F (150°C). Pour the red wine over and continue to roast, uncovered, for 50 to 60 minutes or until it reaches an internal temperature of 140°F (60°C) for rare. Remove the roast from the oven, reserving the liquid, and tent with foil. ■ Melt the margarine in a large heavy skillet. Add the mushrooms and sauté about 5 minutes, until soft and browned. ■ Slice the roast into ½ to ¾ inch (12 to 20 mm) pieces and arrange on a warmed platter. Surround with the mushrooms. Strain the liquid from the roaster and spoon off the fat from the top. Pour over the slices.

One serving… Energy 227cal/951kJ; Fat 12.7g; Protein 24g; Carbohydrate 2g

Eye of the Orient

Water is added to prevent scorching.
Serves 8.

2 lbs.	Eye of round roast	900 g

MARINADE

½ cup	Prepared orange juice	125 mL
½ cup	Sherry	125 mL
¼ cup	Soy sauce	60 mL
2 tsp.	Freshly grated gingerroot	10 mL
¼ cup	Finely chopped onion	60 mL
2 tbsp.	Brown sugar	30 mL
1 tbsp.	Beef bouillon powder	15 mL
1	Garlic clove, crushed	1

■ Pierce the roast several times with a long fork. Place in a deep bowl or sealable plastic bag. Combine the 8 marinade ingredients and pour over the roast. Turn to coat. Cover or seal. Marinate in the refrigerator for 8 to 10 hours or overnight, turning several times. ■ Remove the roast, reserving the marinade. Place on a rack in a medium roaster. ■ Roast, uncovered, in a 500°F (260°C) oven for 30 minutes. Add 1 cup (250 mL) of water to the roasting pan. Reduce heat to 275°F (140°C). Continue to roast, uncovered, for about 1¼ hours or until meat thermometer registers 160°F (70°C) for medium. ■ Strain the reserved marinade. Boil for 2 minutes. Use as is or thicken with 2 tsp. (10 mL) cornstarch mixed with ¼ cup (60 mL) water.

One serving… Energy 184cal/768kJ;
Fat 5.5g; Protein 23g; Carbohydrate 7g

Herbed Beef Tenderloin

Takes only 1 hour to prepare and roast. Use leftover tenderloin in sandwiches. Serves 8.

3 lbs.	Tenderloin roast	1.4 kg
2 tsp.	Olive oil	10 mL
1½ tsp.	Dried thyme	7 mL
1 tsp.	Dried tarragon	5 mL
½ tsp.	Garlic powder	2 mL
1 tsp.	Onion powder	5 mL
1 tsp.	Freshly ground pepper	5 mL
¼ tsp.	Salt	1 mL
2 tsp.	Dried parsley flakes	10 mL

■ If necessary, tuck the thin end of the roast underneath to make the shape as uniform as possible. Tie the tenderloin lengthwise and then crosswise with string to hold the shape. Oil hands with the olive oil and rub the roast all over to coat lightly.
■ Combine the remaining 7 ingredients in a small cup. Spread the seasoning mixture on a piece of waxed paper. Shake the paper to spread evenly. Press the roast down onto the seasonings, rolling to coat all sides. Place on the rack in a broiler pan. ■ Roast in a 425°F (220°C) oven for 45 minutes or until the meat thermometer registers 140°F (60°C) for rare or 160°F (70°C) for medium. Remove from the oven. Tent the roast with foil. Let stand 15 minutes before carving.

One serving… Energy 218cal/913kJ; Fat 11.2g; Protein 27g; Carbohydrate 1g

Smoked Brisket

Chill then shave cooked brisket for use in sandwiches, salads or fajitas. Serves 10.

4 lbs.	Whole brisket, untie string and lay pieces flat	1.8 kg
MARINADE		
5-6	Garlic cloves, minced	5-6
1 tbsp.	Brown sugar	15 mL
2 tbsp.	Worcestershire sauce	30 mL
10 oz.	Condensed beef consommé	284 mL
2 tbsp.	Liquid smoke	30 mL
2 tbsp.	White vinegar	30 mL
1 cup	Soy sauce	250 mL

■ Place the brisket in a large bowl or sealable plastic bag. ■ Combine the 7 marinade ingredients and pour over the roast. Turn to coat. Cover or seal. Marinate in the refrigerator for 24 hours, turning several times. Remove the brisket, discarding the marinade. ■ Place on a rack in a large roaster. Roast, covered, in a 250°F (120°C) oven for 4 hours.

One serving… Energy 232cal/971kJ;
Fat 11.8g; Protein 28g; Carbohydrate 1g

Cranberry Roast

Slice roast thinly across the grain. Heat remaining sauce in roaster and serve as a gravy over rice. Serves 12.

4 lbs.	Eye of round, inside round or sirloin tip roast	1.8 kg
14 oz.	Jellied cranberry sauce	398 mL
2	Green onions, finely chopped	2
¼ cup	Soy sauce	60 mL
2 tbsp.	Freshly grated gingerroot	30 mL

■ Place the roast, fat side up, in the bottom of a medium roaster. Do not place on a rack. Roast, uncovered, in a 500°F (260°C) oven for 30 minutes. ■ Heat the cranberry sauce, onion, soy sauce and ginger in a large saucepan, stirring until smooth. Pour the sauce over the roast, allowing it to drizzle down all sides. ■ Continue to roast, uncovered, in a 275°F (140°C) oven for 25 minutes per lb. (55 minutes per kg) or until the meat thermometer registers 160°F (70°C) for medium. Stir the liquid in the roaster and baste the roast each hour.

One serving… Energy 261cal/1093kJ;
Fat 7.6g; Protein 31g; Carbohydrate 16g

Tangy Beef Roast

Serve thin slices of cooked roast in kaiser buns "buttered" lightly with the Horseradish Spread. Serves 12.

4½ lbs.	Sirloin tip, round or rump roast	2 kg

MARINADE

½ cup	Lemon juice	125 mL
2 tbsp.	Vegetable oil	30 mL
1 tbsp.	Dry mustard powder	15 mL
1 tbsp.	Chopped fresh sweet basil	15 mL
½ tsp.	Salt	2 mL
¼ tsp.	Pepper	1 mL
2	Large garlic cloves, crushed	2

HORSERADISH SPREAD

½ cup	Prepared horseradish	125 mL
1 tsp.	Dry mustard powder	5 mL

■ Pierce the roast several times with a long fork. Place in a deep bowl or sealable plastic bag. Combine the 7 marinade ingredients and pour over the roast. Turn to coat. Cover or seal. Marinate in the refrigerator overnight, turning the bag several times. ■ Remove the roast, discarding the marinade. Place on the rack in a broiler pan. ■ Roast, uncovered, in a 500°F (260°C) oven for 30 minues. Continue to roast, uncovered, in a 275°F (140°C) oven for 25 minutes per lb. (55 minutes per kg) or until the meat thermometer registers 150°F (65°C) for medium-rare. ■ Combine the horseradish and mustard powder in a small bowl. Mix well.

One serving... Energy 219cal/918kJ; Fat 9.9g; Protein 30g; Carbohydrate 1g

Pot Roast Special

Start at least 3 hours ahead. Easy to prepare but needs braising time. Serves 8.

1	Large onion, chopped	1
2 tbsp.	Vegetable oil	30 mL
3 lbs.	Boneless baron of beef (outside round)	1.4 kg
1	Bay leaf	1
1	Orange, grated peel and juice	1
½ tsp.	Ground allspice	2 mL
¼ tsp.	Pepper	1 mL
10 oz.	Condensed beef consommé	284 mL
1 tbsp.	Cornstarch	15 mL
¼ cup	Water	60 mL

■ Sauté the onion in the oil in a Dutch oven until soft. Remove the onion. Add the roast and brown on all sides. Return the onion to the pan. ■ Combine the bay leaf, orange peel, orange juice, allspice, pepper and consommé and pour over the roast and onion. Simmer, covered, for 2½ hours or until the beef is tender. Remove the roast and cover with foil. ■ Strain the liquid. Spoon the fat off the top. Mix the cornstarch and water and stir into the liquid. Blend well. Heat until the gravy is clear and thickened, stirring often.

One serving… Energy 285cal/1194kJ; Fat 13.2g; Protein 35g; Carbohydrate 5g

Texas Pot Roast

Only 15 minutes preparation time but allow 2½ hours for braising. Serves 8.

3½ lbs.	Boneless blade or chuck roast	1.6 kg
1 tbsp.	Vegetable oil	15 mL
2 tbsp.	Taco seasoning mix (35 g pkg.)	30 mL
14 oz.	Canned diced tomatoes, with juice	398 mL
4 oz.	Canned chopped green chilies, with liquid	114 mL
2 tsp.	Beef bouillon powder	10 mL
2 tsp.	Brown sugar	10 mL
6 tbsp.	All-purpose flour	100 mL
½ cup	Water	125 mL

■ Rub the roast with the oil and coat well with the taco seasoning mix. Place on the bottom of a shallow roaster. Broil for 10 minutes per side or until browned. Place in a Dutch oven. ■ Combine the tomato, chilies, bouillon powder and brown sugar in a small bowl. Pour over and around the roast. Simmer, covered, for 2½ hours (or roast, covered, in a 300°F, 150°C oven). Turn the roast after 1½ hours. Remove the roast and cover with foil. ■ Combine the flour and water until smooth. Pour into the liquid in the pan and cook until the sauce is thickened.

One serving… Energy 246cal/1028kJ; Fat 12g; Protein 27g; Carbohydrate 6g

Garlic Roast and Veggies

Stir vegetables occasionally to keep moist. Preparation time 30 minutes plus 2 hours roasting. Serves 8.

2½ lbs.	Sirloin roast	1.1 kg
2	Large garlic cloves, slivered	2
1 tsp.	Dried sweet basil	5 mL
1 tsp.	Dried oregano	5 mL
	Freshly ground pepper, to taste	
1	Large garlic bulb	1
3	Medium baking potatoes, with peel, scrubbed, and quartered	3
2	Medium carrots, sliced diagonally ½ inch (12 mm) thick	2
3	Medium onions, quartered	3
3 tbsp.	Low-fat Italian dressing	50 mL
1	Red pepper, quartered	1
1	Yellow pepper, quartered	1
2	Medium zucchini, with peel, sliced diagonally ¾ inch (2 cm) thick	2
3 tbsp.	Low-fat Italian dressing	50 mL

■ Place the roast on a rack in a large roaster. Make small slits in the roast with a sharp knife and insert the garlic clove slivers evenly over the surface. ■ Combine the basil, oregano and pepper on a piece of waxed paper. Shake the paper to spread evenly. Turn the roast top end down and press onto the seasonings. Place seasoned-end up on the rack. ■ Cut the stem end of the garlic bulb to slice through each clove. Wrap the bulb securely in foil. Place in the roaster. ■ Combine the potato, carrot and onion with the first amount of Italian dressing. Arrange around the roast. ■ Roast, uncovered, in a 325°F (160°C) oven for 30 to 40 minutes per lb. (85 to 110 minutes per kg) or until the meat thermometer registers 160°F (70°C) for medium. Remove the roast to a platter and let stand covered with foil. ■ Combine the peppers and zucchini with the second amount of Italian dressing and add to the vegetables in the roaster. ■ Increase the temperature to 425°F (220°C). Continue roasting vegetables for 20 minutes or until the zucchini is tender-crisp. Remove the foilwrapped garlic and squeeze the garlic through the cut end over the roasted vegetables. Toss lightly to combine.

One serving... Energy 223cal/932kJ; Fat 6.9g; Protein 25g; Carbohydrate 15g

Ruby-Glazed Roast Beef

Only 5 minutes preparation time but allow about 3½ hours for braising. Serves 8.

3 lbs.	Inside round or eye of round roast	1.4 kg
1 cup	Red currant jelly	250 mL
½ tsp.	Ground ginger	2 mL
¼ cup	Chopped sun-dried tomatoes, softened in boiling water 5 minutes before chopping	60 mL
1 tsp.	Dried Italian seasoning	5 mL
1 tbsp.	Cornstarch	15 mL
¼ cup	Cold water	60 mL

■ Place the roast fat side up on a rack in a small roaster. Roast, uncovered, in a 500°F (260°C) oven for 30 minutes. Heat the jelly, ginger, tomato and herb seasoning in a small saucepan. Pour the sauce over the roast. ■ Continue to roast, uncovered, in a 275° (140°C) oven for 25 minutes per lb. (55 minutes per kg) or until the meat thermometer registers 160°F (70°C) for medium. Baste several times with the sauce. ■ Mix the cornstarch with the water and stir into the liquid in the roaster. Heat and stir until thickened.

One serving… Energy 462cal/1932kJ; Fat 10.7g; Protein 45g; Carbohydrate 46g

Savory Rib Roast

Substitute a prime rib roast, if desired. Only 5 minutes to prepare but allow 3½ hours for roasting. Serves 12.

6 lbs.	Standing rib roast	2.7 kg
1 tbsp.	Ground thyme	15 mL
1 tsp.	Dried rosemary, crushed	5 mL
1 tsp.	Ground sage	5 mL
1 tsp.	Salt	5 mL
1 tsp.	Freshly ground pepper	5 mL

■ Place the roast, fat side up, on a rack in a large roaster. Combine the seasonings and rub on the surface of the roast. ■ Roast, uncovered, in a 325°F (160°C) oven for 35 minutes per lb. (75 minutes per kg) for rare; 45 minutes per lb. (100 minutes per kg) for medium; 55 minutes per lb. (120 minutes per kg) for well-done. ■ Let stand 10 minutes before carving.

One serving… Energy 237cal/994kJ; Fat 11.6g; Protein 31g; Carbohydrate trace

Seasoned Sirloin

Preparation time only 10 minutes plus 2½ hours for roasting. Serves 8.

3 lbs.	Sirloin roast	1.4 kg
4	Garlic cloves, minced	4
2 tsp.	Olive oil	10 mL
1 tsp.	Paprika	5 mL
1 tsp.	Freshly ground pepper	5 mL
1 tsp.	Onion powder	5 mL

■ Place the roast on a rack in a medium roaster. Combine the 5 remaining ingredients in a small bowl. Mix into a paste. Spread the paste over the surface of the roast. ■ Roast, uncovered, in a 325°F (160°C) oven for 30 to 40 minutes per pound (65 to 85 minutes per kg) or until the meat thermometer registers 160°F (70°C) for medium. Let the roast stand for 10 minutes before carving.

One serving… 225cal/939kJ; Fat 9.9g; Protein 31g; Carbohydrate 1g

C H A P T E R   7

Salads

Far East Beef Salad, page 125

Kiwi, Beef and Pasta Salad

Serve this salad warm or cold. Serves 4.

MARINADE

3	Ripe kiwis, peeled and mashed	3
⅓ cup	Lime juice	75 mL
⅓ cup	Water	75 mL
1 tbsp.	Granulated sugar	15 mL
2	Garlic cloves, minced	2
1	Small onion, finely chopped	1
1	Gingerroot, 1 inch (2.5 cm), finely chopped	1
1 tsp.	Dried tarragon	5 mL
½ tsp.	Salt	2 mL
1 tsp.	Lemon pepper	5 mL
1 lb.	Round or sirloin tip steak, ¾ inch (2 cm) thick	454 g
3 cups	Fusilli or shell pasta, uncooked	750 mL
12	Cherry tomatoes, halved	12

GARNISH

Kiwi, peeled and sliced

Star fruit, sliced

■ Combine the 10 marinade ingredients. Place the steak in a shallow dish or sealable plastic bag and pour the marinade over top. Turn to coat. Cover or seal. Marinate in the refrigerator for 30 to 45 minutes, turning the steak once. ■ Remove the steak, reserving the marinade. Cut the steak into thin slices. Brown quickly in a non-stick skillet. ■ Boil the reserved marinade in a small saucepan for 5 to 10 minutes. ■ Cook the pasta according to package directions. Drain. Combine the pasta, marinade and tomatoes in a large bowl. Toss to mix. Arrange the steak strips over the pasta. ■ Garnish with kiwi and star fruit slices.

One serving… Energy 357cal/1494kJ;
Fat 5.3g; Protein 29g; Carbohydrate 49g

Steak 'n' Veggie Pasta Salad

Marinate the steak and prepare all the vegetables the day before. Serves 6.

1½ lbs.	Round or sirloin tip steak	680 g

MARINADE

1 tbsp.	Olive oil	15 mL
1 tbsp.	Red wine vinegar	15 mL
1 tbsp.	Condensed beef broth	15 mL
2	Garlic cloves, minced	2
	Freshly ground pepper, to taste	
2 cups	Rotini pasta, uncooked	500 mL
½ cup	Small cauliflower florets	125 mL
½ cup	Small broccoli florets	125 mL
2	Carrots, cut julienne	2
2	Green onions, thinly sliced	2
½	Green pepper, cut julienne	½
½	Red pepper, cut julienne	½
1 cup	Low-fat Italian or Caesar dressing	250 mL
½ tsp.	Salt	2 mL
	Freshly ground pepper, to taste	

GARNISH

Grated Parmesan cheese

■ Pierce the steak with a fork at regular intervals and place in a shallow dish or sealable plastic bag. Combine the 5 marinade ingredients and pour over the steak. Turn to coat well. Cover or seal. Marinate in the refrigerator for 8 hours or overnight, turning several times. Remove the steak and discard the marinade.
■ Broil the steak for 4 to 5 minutes per side or to desired doneness. Cool completely. Cut in very thin diagonal slices across the grain. ■ Cook the pasta according to package directions. Drain and rinse in cold water. Blanch the cauliflower, broccoli and carrot. Cool immediately in ice water. Pat dry. ■ Combine the steak, pasta and vegetables in a large bowl. Toss with the dressing, salt and pepper. Marinate in the refrigerator for at least 1 hour to blend the flavors. ■ Sprinkle with Parmesan cheese.

One serving… Energy 306cal/1280kJ; Fat 8.3g; Protein 27g; Carbohydrate 30g

Beef and Spinach Salad

Prepare the vegetables while the steak is cooking. Serves 4.

1 tbsp.	Vegetable oil	15 mL
2	Garlic cloves, minced	2
½ tsp.	Salt	2 mL
½ tsp.	Freshly ground pepper	2 mL
1 lb.	Top sirloin steak, ¾ inch (2 cm) thick	454 g
10 cups	Torn fresh spinach	2.5 L
1 cup	Grated carrot	250 mL
1½ cups	Sliced fresh mushrooms	375 mL
⅓ cup	Low-fat creamy dressing (your favorite)	75 mL

GARNISH

Croutons

Imitation bacon bits

■ Combine the oil, garlic, salt and pepper. Spread over both sides of the steak. Heat a non-stick skillet until hot. Cook the steak for 5 to 7 minutes on each side or to desired doneness. Trim off the fat. Cut the steak lengthwise in half and then crosswise into ¼ inch (6 mm) slices. ■ Toss the spinach, carrot and mushrooms with the dressing in a large serving bowl. Arrange the sliced beef on top. ■ Sprinkle with croutons and bacon bits. Serve immediately.

One serving… Energy 257cal/1077kJ; Fat 11.2g; Protein 28g; Carbohydrate 13g

Minty Beef Salad

Do the chopping and cutting while steak is marinating. Total time is 45 minutes. Serves 8.

DRESSING

2	Limes, grated peel and juice	2
3 tbsp.	Minced gingerroot	50 mL
2 tbsp.	Chopped fresh coriander (cilantro)	30 mL
1 cup	Packed fresh mint leaves	250 mL
1 tsp.	Brown sugar	5 mL
1 tbsp.	Soy sauce	15 mL
½ cup	Water	125 mL
½ cup	Olive oil	125 mL
½ tsp.	Sesame oil	2 mL
¾ lb.	Flank steak	340 g
2	Medium heads butter lettuce, torn	2
1 cup	Bean sprouts	250 mL
2 cups	Diced cantaloupe, in ½ inch (12 mm) cubes	500 mL
½ cup	Coarsely chopped salted peanuts	125 mL

■ Process the 9 dressing ingredients in a blender until smooth. ■ Place the steak in a shallow dish or sealable plastic bag and pour in ¹/₂ the dressing. Turn to coat well. Cover or seal. Marinate in the refrigerator for 30 minutes, turning once. ■ Remove the steak to a broiler pan and discard the marinade. ■ Broil for 5 minutes per side or to desired doneness. Cool. Cut the steak diagonally across the grain into thin slices. ■ Combine the lettuce, bean sprouts, cantaloupe and peanuts. Toss lightly with the remaining ½ dressing. Arrange the cooked steak over top.

One serving… Energy 174cal/1009kJ; Fat 17.5g; Protein 13g; Carbohydrate 10g

Peachy Beef Salad

Uses leftover cooked beef. Quick to prepare.
Serves 6.

14 oz.	Canned sliced peaches, juice reserved	398 mL
1	Head romaine lettuce, torn into pieces	1
1½ cups	Strips cooked lean beef	375 mL
1	Medium-ripe avocado, sliced	1

DRESSING

¼ cup	Low-fat Italian dressing	60 mL
2 tbsp.	Sweet and sour barbecue sauce	30 mL
¼ cup	Reserved peach juice	60 mL
	Freshly ground pepper, to taste	

GARNISH

Cherry tomatoes
Toasted almonds

■ Toss the peaches, lettuce, beef and avocado together in a large bowl. ■ Combine the 4 dressing ingredients and toss lightly with the lettuce mixture. Season with pepper. ■ Garnish with cherry tomatoes and almonds.

One serving… Energy 167cal/697kJ;
Fat 7.6g; Protein 13g; Carbohydrate 13g

Beef Tabbouleh

The bulgur adds a nice crunch. Ready in 10 minutes. Serves 6.

1 cup	Bulgur	250 mL
2 cups	Boiling water	500 mL
2	Plum tomatoes, seeded and diced	2
½ cup	Very thinly sliced red onion	125 mL
¼ cup	Finely chopped fresh mint	60 mL
3 tbsp.	Finely chopped fresh parsley	50 mL
2	Green onions, finely chopped	2
1 cup	Finely chopped cooked lean beef	250 mL
1 tbsp.	Olive oil	15 mL
3 tbsp.	Lemon juice	50 mL
¼ tsp.	Ground cumin	1 mL
¼ tsp.	Ground coriander	1 mL
⅛ tsp.	Hot pepper sauce	0.5 mL
1 tsp.	Salt	5 mL
¼ tsp.	Lemon pepper	1 mL

■ Place the bulgur in a bowl and pour the boiling water over. Let stand for 30 minutes. Drain any excess water. ■ Combine the remaining ingredients and toss with the bulgur. Chill for 30 minutes to blend the flavors.

One serving… Energy 169cal/708kJ; Fat 4.2g; Protein 11g; Carbohydrate 24g

Mango Tango Salad

Marinate the steak overnight. Prepare the rest of the salad in the morning. Serves 4.

1 lb.	Inside round or sirloin tip steak	454 g
½ cup	Dry red wine	125 mL
2 cups	Penne, fusilli or rigatoni pasta, uncooked	500 mL
1 cup	Hot mango chutney	250 mL
2 tsp.	Vegetable oil	10 mL
1 tsp.	Sesame oil	5 mL
¼ cup	Lemon juice	60 mL
1½ cups	Frozen peas	375 mL
1	Large carrot, cut julienne	1
½ cup	Diced ripe mango	125 mL
2 tbsp.	Toasted sesame seeds	30 mL

■ Lightly score both surfaces of the steak with a sharp knife. Place in a shallow dish or sealable plastic bag and pour in the wine. Turn to coat well. Cover or seal. Marinate in the refrigerator for a minimum of 2 hours, turning several times. Remove the steak and discard the wine. ■ Broil the steak for 5 to 6 minutes per side or to desired doneness. Thinly slice the steak across the grain. ■ Cook the pasta according to package directions. Rinse under cold water and drain well. ■ Blend the chutney with the oils and lemon juice. Combine with the pasta, steak, peas, carrot and mango. Refrigerate for 3 to 4 hours to blend the flavors. ■ Toss with the toasted sesame seeds just before serving.

One serving… Energy 470cal/1968kJ;
Fat 11g; Protein 33g; Carbohydrate 58g

123

Summertime Salad

Make the dressing the day before. Cover and refrigerate until ready to use. Shake well. Serves 6 as a luncheon meal.

3 cups	Julienned strips cooked lean beef	750 mL
1 cup	Sliced steamed green beans	250 mL
½ cup	Sliced English cucumber, with peel	125 mL
1½ cups	Diced celery	375 mL
½ cup	Diced green pepper	125 mL
1 lb.	New baby potatoes, boiled and diced	454 g
¼ cup	Finely chopped green onion	60 mL
3 tbsp.	Chopped fresh parsley	50 mL

DRESSING

⅓ cup	Olive oil	75 mL
2 tbsp.	Balsamic vinegar	30 mL
¾ tsp.	Salt	4 mL
1	Small garlic clove, minced	1
1½ tsp.	Dijon mustard	7 mL
¼ tsp.	Dried tarragon	1 mL

Mixed salad greens

GARNISH

Chopped fresh parsley
Tomatoes, cut into wedges
Hard-boiled eggs, sliced

■ Combine the first 8 ingredients in a large bowl. ■ Combine the next 6 dressing ingredients and toss with the vegetable mixture. Refrigerate at least 1 hour to blend flavors. ■ Serve on a bed of salad greens. ■ Garnish with chopped parsley, tomato wedges and egg slices.

One serving…Energy 324cal/1354kJ; Fat 17.9g; Protein 25g; Carbohydrate 17g

Far East Beef Salad

Prepare the dressing and vegetables while the steak is broiling. Serves 4.

1 lb.	Sirloin or round steak	454 g
¼ cup	Low-fat French dressing	60 mL
¾ cup	Low-fat French dressing	175 mL
¼ cup	Soy sauce	60 mL
1½ tbsp.	Brown sugar, packed	25 mL
	Reserved steak drippings	
¼ tsp.	Crushed chilies	1 mL
4 cups	Thinly shredded savoy cabbage	1 L
1	Small red onion, finely sliced	1
2 tbsp.	Toasted sesame seeds	30 mL
2 tbsp.	Chopped fresh cilantro (coriander)	30 mL

GARNISH

Cantaloupe slices

■ Coat the steak with the first amount of dressing. Place on a broiler pan and broil for 3 to 4 minutes per side, or to desired doneness. Cut the steak across the grain into thin slices and reserve the drippings. Set aside. ■ Heat the second amount of dressing in a medium saucepan with the soy sauce, brown sugar and reserved drippings. Add the steak slices and chilies. ■ Arrange the cabbage and onion slices in a large bowl or on 4 salad plates and cover with the warm steak and dressing. Sprinkle with the sesame seeds and cilantro. Surround with cantaloupe slices. Serve immediately.

One serving… Energy 322cal/1348kJ; Fat 13.6g; Protein 27g; Carbohydrate 25g

Apple and Beef Salad

Use unpeeled boiled new potatoes, halved or quartered. Serves 6 for lunch.

3 cups	Cooked lean beef, cut into ½ inch (12 mm) cubes	750 mL
3 cups	Coarsely diced cooked potato	750 mL
½ cup	Finely chopped celery	125 mL
1	Medium green pepper, finely chopped	1
1 cup	Grated colby cheese	250 mL
2	Medium apples, diced into ½ inch (12 mm) pieces	2
1 tsp.	Lemon juice	5 mL

DILL DRESSING

½ cup	Light salad dressing (or mayonnaise)	125 mL
¼ cup	1% milk	60 mL
1 tsp.	Dill weed	5 mL
½ tsp.	Salt	2 mL
	Pepper, to taste	

GARNISH

Paprika

■ Combine the first 5 ingredients in a large bowl. Place the diced apple in a small bowl and toss with the lemon juice. Add to the beef mixture. ■ Combine the salad dressing, milk, dill weed, salt and pepper in a small bowl. Add to the beef mixture and toss gently. ■ Sprinkle with paprika.

One serving…Energy 374cal/1563kJ;
Fat 17.1g; Protein 28g; Carbohydrate 27g

Artichoke Toss

Serve warm or cold. Serves 4.

½ cup	Low-fat French dressing	125 mL
2 tbsp.	Vegetable oil	30 mL
2	Garlic cloves, minced	2
1 tsp.	Ground cumin	5 mL
1 lb.	Sirloin, strip loin or inside round steak	454 g
½ cup	Sliced fresh mushrooms	125 mL
½	Red pepper, cut into slivers	½
½	Yellow pepper, cut into slivers	½
14 oz.	Canned artichoke hearts, drained and quartered	398 mL
4-8	Lettuce leaves	4-8

■ Combine the first 4 ingredients. Reserve and set aside ¼ cup (60 mL). ■ Pierce the steak with a fork several times. Lay in a shallow dish and pour the dressing mixture over top. Turn to coat well. Cover and marinate in the refrigerator for 1½ hours. ■ Broil the steak for 5 to 6 minutes per side or to desired doneness. Thinly slice across the grain. ■ Combine the mushrooms and peppers with the reserved dressing mixture. Place on a broiler pan and broil for 2 minutes. Toss with the quartered artichokes. ■ Arrange the lettuce leaves on individual plates or line a shallow bowl and top with the beef slices and tossed vegetables.

One serving… Energy 242cal/1010kJ;
Fat 9.7g; Protein 26g; Carbohydrate 14g

CHAPTER 8

Sandwiches

Beef and Avocado Sandwiches, page 138

Mexican Flatbread Pizza

As a variation, omit the flatbread and serve in taco shells or wrapped in tortillas. Cuts into 8 wedges.

1 lb.	Minute steaks or fast-fry steaks, ¼ inch (6 mm) thick	454 g
½ cup	Chunky salsa (mild, medium or hot)	125 mL
2 tbsp.	Lime juice	30 mL
1	Flatbread or prebaked pizza crust, 12 inch (30 cm)	1
½ cup	Chunky salsa (mild, medium or hot)	125 mL
¼ cup	Grated Monterey Jack cheese	60 mL
¼ cup	Grated medium Cheddar cheese	60 mL

■ Marinate the steak in the first amount of salsa and lime juice for 15 minutes. ■ Place the flatbread in a warm oven while preparing the steak. Remove the steak, discarding the marinade. Cook the steak in a non-stick skillet for 2 minutes per side or to desired doneness. Cut into thin strips. ■ Spread the flatbread or pizza crust with the second amount of salsa. Top with the steak and sprinkle with the cheeses. Broil for 2 minutes or until the cheese is melted.

One wedge… Energy 237cal/990kJ; Fat 7.3g; Protein 18g; Carbohydrate 24g

Gyro Sandwiches

Prepare and assemble in 10 minutes. Makes 6 pita sandwiches.

GYRO SAUCE

¾ cup	Light salad dressing (or mayonnaise)	175 mL
¼ cup	1% milk	60 mL
2	Garlic cloves, minced	2
1 tsp.	Dried oregano	5 mL
¼ tsp.	Pepper	1 mL
3	Pita breads (7 inch, 17.5 cm), cut in half	3

FILLING

¾ lb.	Thinly sliced lean cooked or deli beef	340 g
1 cup	Shredded lettuce	250 mL
1 cup	Chopped tomato	250 mL
½ cup	Thinly sliced red onion	125 mL
¼ cup	Sliced pitted ripe olives	60 mL

■ Combine the 5 Gyro Sauce ingredients in a medium bowl. Chill. ■ Fill the pita "pockets" with the beef, lettuce, tomato, onion and olives. ■ Spoon the Gyro Sauce into each filled pita half.

One pita sandwich… Energy 287cal/1200kJ; Fat 11.6g; Protein 20g; Carbohydrate 25g

Mediterranean Beef Salad Sandwiches

Make the salad the day before but remove from the marinade after 2 hours and refrigerate overnight. Makes 12 pita sandwiches.

½ lb.	Cooked lean beef, cut in thin strips	225 g
1 cup	Broccoli florets, blanched and put in ice water	250 mL
⅔ cup	Sliced English cucumber, with peel	150 mL
⅔ cup	Sliced celery	150 mL
⅔ cup	Sliced red pepper	150 mL
¼ cup	Halved pitted ripe olives	60 mL
10	Pickled onions, sliced	10
½ cup	Crumbled feta cheese	125 mL
	Freshly ground pepper, to taste	
½ cup	Low-fat Italian dressing	125 mL
6	Pita breads (7 inch, 17.5 cm), cut in half	6

■ Combine the first 8 ingredients and toss together. Season with pepper. Add the dressing and toss together well. Marinate in the refrigerator for at least 1 hour to blend the flavors. ■ Divide the salad among the pita "pockets" and serve.

One pita sandwich… Energy 143cal/597kJ; Fat 2.5g; Protein 9g; Carbohydrate 21g

Beef Vegetable Sandwiches

Ready in 20 minutes. Uses leftover cooked beef.
Makes 4 sandwiches.

½ cup	Plain yogurt	125 mL
½ cup	Grated carrot	125 mL
1 tbsp.	Finely chopped onion	15 mL
½ tsp.	Dried sweet basil	2 mL
4	Kaiser buns	4
4	Lettuce leaves	4
1	Large tomato, thinly sliced	1
8 oz.	Cooked lean beef, thinly sliced	250 g
½	Medium cucumber, peeled and thinly sliced	½
¼ cup	Grated medium Cheddar cheese	60 mL
1 cup	Alfalfa sprouts	250 mL
	Salt, to taste	
	Pepper, to taste	

■ Combine the yogurt, carrot, onion, and basil in a small bowl. Stir. Set aside. ■ Slice the buns in half horizontally. Layer the bottom halves with the lettuce, tomato, beef, cucumber, cheese and sprouts. Sprinkle with salt and pepper. Spoon ¼ cup (60 mL) of the yogurt mixture over top of the sprouts. Cover with the top halves of the buns.

One sandwich… Energy 300cal/1254kJ;
Fat 8.2g; Protein 28g; Carbohydrate 37g

Speedy Fajitas

Only 20 minutes from start to finish when you buy pre-cut stir-fry strips. Makes 8 fajitas.

1 tbsp.	Lime juice	15 mL
1 tbsp.	Chili powder	15 mL
1 tsp.	Dried oregano	5 mL
½ tsp.	Garlic powder	2 mL
	Freshly ground pepper, to taste	
1 lb.	Beef stir-fry strips	454 g
2 cups	Sliced fresh mushrooms	500 mL
1	Medium red or green pepper, cut in strips	1
4	Green onions, cut in 1 inch (2.5 cm) pieces	4
2 tsp.	Vegetable oil	10 mL
8	Flour tortillas (10 inch, 25 cm)	8
½ cup	Salsa (mild, medium or hot)	125 mL

■ Mix the first 5 ingredients together in a medium bowl. Add the beef strips and stir to coat. Set aside. ■ Sauté the mushrooms, pepper strips and green onion in the oil in a non-stick skillet for 2 to 3 minutes. Remove the vegetables to a bowl. ■ Wrap the tortillas in a damp tea towel and warm in the oven. ■ Stir-fry the beef strips, along with the marinade, in a non-stick skillet for 5 minutes or until browned. Add the beef mixture to the vegetable mixture. Divide the beef and vegetable mixture between the 8 warmed tortillas (½ cup, 125 mL filling per tortilla). Put 1 tbsp. (15 mL) salsa on each tortilla. Fold up the bottom and then fold in the 2 sides, envelope style, leaving the top open.

One fajita… Energy 242cal/1012kJ;
Fat 6.2g; Protein 18g; Carbohydrate 29g

Pita Pizzas

Cut into small wedges to use as an appetizer. Makes 8 individual pizzas.

½ lb.	Lean ground beef	225 g
⅓ cup	Finely diced onion	75 mL
¼ tsp.	Ground oregano	1 mL
¼ tsp.	Salt	1 mL
¼ tsp.	Garlic powder	1 mL
8	Whole wheat pita breads (7 inch, 17.5 cm)	8
7½ oz.	Tomato sauce or pizza sauce	213 mL
1 cup	Finely chopped fresh mushrooms	250 mL
1½ cups	Finely diced green pepper	375 mL
2 cups	Grated part skim mozzarella cheese	500 mL

■ Scramble-fry the beef, onion, oregano, salt and garlic powder in a non-stick skillet until the onion is soft and the beef is no longer pink. Drain.
■ Flatten the pita breads using a rolling pin. Spread each pita bread with about 1½ tbsp. (25 mL) tomato sauce. Sprinkle with 3 tbsp. (50 mL) beef mixture, 2 tbsp. (30 mL) mushrooms and 2 tbsp. (30 mL) green pepper. Sprinkle ¼ cup (60 mL) cheese over top. ■ Broil 6 to 8 inches (15 to 20 cm) from the heat until the edges are crusty and the cheese is melted. Cut into quarters to serve.

One pizza… Energy 304cal/1270kJ;
Fat 8.1g; Protein 19g; Carbohydrate 38g

Surprise Burgers

Prepare and cook in 30 minutes. There's a surprise in the middle! Makes 4 burgers.

1 lb.	Lean ground beef	454 g
1	Large egg	1
3 tbsp.	Chopped cooked spinach, squeezed dry	50 mL
1 tbsp.	Grated onion	15 mL
½ tsp.	Salt	2 mL
	Freshly ground pepper, to taste	
3 tbsp.	Grated medium Cheddar cheese	50 mL
	Light salad dressing (or mayonnaise)	
	Ketchup	
4	Kaiser or other hamburger buns, split and toasted	4
4	Slices ripe tomato	4

■ Combine the first 6 ingredients in a medium bowl. Divide into 4 large portions and 4 small portions. Form the large portions into patties. Make an indentation in the center of each patty and fill each with ¼ of the cheese. ■ Flatten the small portion of the beef mixture and seal over top of the cheese. Broil or barbecue the patties for 10 minutes or until no longer pink inside. ■ Spread salad dressing and ketchup on each toasted bun. Top with the burger and tomato slice.

One burger… Energy 338cal/1414kJ;
Fat 13.9g; Protein 27g; Carbohydrate 25g

Barbecue Beefwiches

A fast lunch. Ready in 10 minutes. Doubles or triples easily. Makes 2 sandwiches.

¼ cup	Barbecue sauce	60 mL
¼ cup	Salsa (mild, medium or hot)	60 mL
½ lb.	Thinly sliced cooked lean beef, cut into strips	225 g
2	Large hamburger buns, cut in half	2
	Bread and butter pickles	

■ Heat the barbecue sauce and salsa in a non-stick skillet. Add the beef strips and mix well to coat. Heat gently until hot. ■ Toast the cut surfaces of the buns. Top with the beef mixture. Arrange the pickles over top. Top with the other bun half. Wrap in foil and heat in a 350°F (175°C) oven for 10 minutes.

One sandwich… Energy 363cal/1520kJ;
Fat 9.1g; Protein 37g; Carbohydrate 31g

Mexi-Beef Pitas

A great kids' lunch or after school snack. Make the filling ahead and keep on hand. Makes 10 mini pita sandwiches.

10	Pita breads (3 inch, 7.5 cm)	10
FILLING		
1 lb.	Lean ground beef	454 g
½ cup	Finely chopped onion	125 mL
14 oz.	Canned pinto beans, drained	398 mL
½ cup	Diced green pepper	125 mL
¼ cup	Diced red pepper	60 mL
2 tsp.	Chili powder	10 mL
1 tsp.	Salt	5 mL
¾ cup	Grated Monterey Jack cheese	175 mL

■ Place the pita bread in a 300°F (150°C) oven to warm. ■ Scramble-fry the beef in a non-stick skillet until no longer pink. Drain. ■ Add the next 6 ingredients. Mix well. Heat thoroughly for 2 to 3 minutes. ■ Remove the pita breads from the oven. Make a slit in the seam of each pita and open the "pocket". Spoon the filling into the warmed pitas. ■ Sprinkle with the cheese. Place on an ungreased baking sheet and return to the oven until the cheese is melted.

One pita sandwich… Energy 190cal/794kJ; Fat 6.8g; Protein 14g; Carbohydrate 18g

Beef and Avocado Sandwiches

Serve immediately before avocado starts to turn color. Makes 8 sandwiches.

1 cup	Packed fresh sweet basil leaves	250 mL
¼ cup	Coarsely chopped fresh parsley, tough stems removed	60 mL
3	Garlic cloves, halved	3
¼ cup	Coarsely chopped onion	60 mL
1	Ripe avocado, peeled and halved	1
2 tbsp.	Lemon juice	30 mL
½ tsp.	Salt	2 mL
	Freshly ground pepper, to taste	
3 tbsp.	Olive oil	50 mL
8	Fresh Italian or kaiser buns, cut in half	8
1 lb.	Deli or cooked lean beef, very thinly sliced	454 g
2	Large tomatoes, sliced	2
8	Red or green leafy lettuce leaves	8
	Salt, to taste	
	Freshly ground pepper, to taste	

■ Combine the basil leaves, parsley, garlic and onion in a food processor. Process, scraping down sides occasionally, until the herbs are finely minced. ■ Add the avocado, lemon juice, salt, pepper and olive oil. Process until smooth. Remove the mixture to a bowl. Cover. Refrigerate for 30 minutes to blend the flavors. ■ Spread the avocado-basil mixture on the bottom half of each bun. Layer the beef, tomato and lettuce on top of the spread. Season with salt and pepper. Cover with the tops of the buns.

One sandwich… Energy 356cal/1491kJ; Fat 13.8g; Protein 23g; Carbohydrate 36g

Beef Benedict

Multiply the recipe for as many people as serving. Serves 1.

¼ cup	Béarnaise Sauce, page 12	60 mL
4 oz.	Rib-eye or sirloin steak	125 g
½	English muffin, toasted	½
1	Large egg, poached	1
	Paprika	

■ Prepare the Béarnaise Sauce. Keep warm. ■ Broil, grill or pan fry the steak to desired doneness. Cut into thin strips and pile onto the English muffin. Top with the poached egg and Béarnaise Sauce. Sprinkle with paprika.

One serving... Energy 381cal/1592kJ; Fat 11.4g; Protein 37g; Carbohydrate 30g

139

CHAPTER 9

Soups

Spicy Beef and Rice Soup, page 147

Bok Choy Beef Soup

Make the rest of the soup while the beef is marinating. Makes 8 cups (2 L).

½ lb.	Flank steak	225 g
1 tsp.	Cornstarch	5 mL
½ tsp.	Freshly grated gingerroot	2 mL
½ tsp.	Vegetable or sesame oil	2 mL
1 tbsp.	Soy sauce	15 mL
Pinch	Crushed chilies	Pinch
3 x 10 oz.	Condensed beef broth	3 x 284 mL
3 cups	Water	750 mL
1 cup	Julienned carrot	250 mL
½ cup	Finely slivered onion	125 mL
6	Large stalks of bok choy, cut into ½ x 2 inch (1.2 x 5 cm) pieces	6

GARNISH

Thinly sliced green onion

Toasted sesame seeds

■ Slice the steak with the grain into 2 inch (5 cm) strips. Cut the strips against the grain into ⅛ inch (3 mm) slivers. Beef should be very finely cut. ■ Combine the cornstarch, ginger, oil, soy sauce and chilies in a small bowl. Add the beef strips and stir to combine. Cover and refrigerate for 30 minutes. ■ Pour the broth and water into a large saucepan and boil. Add the carrot and onion. Cover and simmer for 15 minutes. Stir in the marinated beef and bok choy and allow soup to boil, uncovered, for 3 minutes. ■ Garnish each serving with green onion and sesame seeds.

One cup (250 mL)… Energy 95cal/399kJ; Fat 2.4g; Protein 12g; Carbohydrate 6g

Minestrone

Adjust the seasonings and hot pepper sauce for a spicier flavor. Makes 13 cups (3.25 L).

1 lb.	Lean ground beef	454 g
3	Garlic cloves, minced	3
1	Large onion, chopped	1
2	Large celery stalks, chopped	2
6 cups	Water	1.5 L
2½ tbsp.	Beef bouillon powder	37 mL
2	Medium carrots, quartered lengthwise and sliced	2
1	Medium zucchini, with peel, quartered lengthwise and sliced	1
2	Bay leaves	2
¼ cup	Finely chopped fresh sweet basil	60 mL
1 tsp.	Dried oregano	5 mL
1 tbsp.	Finely chopped fresh parsley	15 mL
¼ tsp.	Pepper	1 mL
½ tsp.	Hot pepper sauce	2 mL
28 oz.	Canned tomatoes, with juice, chopped	796 mL
1 cup	Orzo pasta, uncooked	250 mL
14 oz.	Canned kidney beans, with liquid	398 mL

GARNISH

Freshly grated Parmesan cheese

■ Scramble-fry the beef in a Dutch oven until no pink remains. Drain. Add the garlic, onion, and celery. Sauté, stirring frequently, until the onion and celery are soft. ■ Add the next 11 ingredients. Bring the mixture to a boil. Reduce the heat. Cover and simmer for 45 minutes or until the vegetables are tender. ■ Add the pasta and beans. Simmer for 10 minutes more or until the pasta is cooked. Discard the bay leaf. ■ Sprinkle individual servings with Parmesan cheese.

One cup (250 mL)… Energy 143cal/597kJ; Fat 3.5g; Protein 10g; Carbohydrate 18g

Black Bean Soup

Ready in 30 minutes. Excellent the next day.
Makes 8 cups (2 L).

½ lb.	Lean ground beef	225 g
1	Large onion, chopped	1
3	Garlic cloves, minced	3
¼ tsp.	Dried oregano	1 mL
¼ tsp.	Dried thyme	1 mL
¼ tsp.	Ground cumin	1 mL
¼ tsp.	Cayenne pepper	1 mL
½ tsp.	Salt	2 mL
2 x 19 oz.	Canned black beans, with liquid	2 x 540 mL
2 x 10 oz.	Condensed beef broth	2 x 284 mL
½ cup	Grated carrot	125 mL
10 oz.	Water	284 mL

GARNISH

Non-fat sour cream

Finely diced red onion

■ Scramble-fry the beef with the onion and garlic in a Dutch oven until the beef is browned and the onion is soft. Drain. Add the seasonings. Sauté for 2 minutes. ■ Purée the black beans with the beef broth until smooth. Pour into the beef mixture. Add the carrot and water. Let the soup simmer for 10 minutes to soften the carrot and blend the flavors. ■ Ladle the soup into 8 bowls. ■ Garnish with a swirl of sour cream and a sprinkle of red onion.

One cup (250 mL)... Energy 211cal/885kJ;
Fat 3g; Protein 18g; Carbohydrate 29g

Oriental Beef and Cabbage Soup

Easy and quick. Ready in 25 minutes. Makes 8 cups (2 L).

¾ lb.	Round steak, thinly sliced into ¼ x ¾ inch (0.6 x 2 cm) strips	340 g
2 tbsp.	Sherry	30 mL
1 tbsp.	Vegetable oil	15 mL
1 tbsp.	Soy sauce	15 mL
½ tsp.	Cornstarch	2 mL
2 x 10 oz.	Condensed beef broth	2 x 284 mL
2 x 10 oz.	Water	2 x 284 mL
1 tsp.	Ground ginger	5 mL
½ tsp.	Garlic powder	2 mL
¼ tsp.	Freshly ground pepper	1 mL
1½ cups	Coarsely shredded bok choy or regular cabbage	375 mL
½ cup	Chopped onion	125 mL

GARNISH

Thinly sliced green onion

■ Combine the beef strips with the next 4 ingredients in a small bowl and stir well. Set aside. ■ Bring the broth, water and seasonings to a boil in a large saucepan or Dutch oven. Reduce the heat and simmer for 10 minutes. ■ Add the bok choy and onion and bring to a boil. Reduce heat and simmer for 2 minutes. ■ Add the beef mixture and simmer for 3 to 4 minutes or until the beef is cooked. ■ Garnish each serving with green onion.

One cup (250 mL)… Energy 94cal/393kJ; Fat 3.4g; Protein 12g; Carbohydrate 3g

Meatball Vegetable Soup

Garnish individual servings with Parmesan cheese, if desired. Makes 8 cups (2 L).

1 lb.	Lean ground beef	454 g
1	Large egg	1
1 tsp.	Dried oregano	5 mL
1	Small garlic clove, minced	1
½ tsp.	Salt	2 mL
1	Medium onion, thinly sliced	1
1 tsp.	Vegetable oil	5 mL
2 tbsp.	Beef bouillon powder	30 mL
6 cups	Boiling water	1.5 L
½ cup	Thinly sliced carrot	125 mL
½ cup	Thinly sliced celery	125 mL
1 tbsp.	Chopped fresh parsley	15 mL
1½ tsp.	Chopped fresh sweet basil	7 mL
2 tsp.	Worcestershire sauce	10 mL
	Salt, to taste	
	Pepper, to taste	

■ Combine the beef with the next 4 ingredients and form into 1 inch (2.5 cm) balls. Brown on all sides in a non-stick skillet. Drain. Remove from the skillet. ■ Sauté the onion in the oil in the same skillet until soft and starting to brown. ■ Dissolve the bouillon powder in the boiling water in a large saucepan or Dutch oven. Add the next 5 ingredients and bring to a boil. Reduce the heat and add the onion and meatballs. Cover and simmer for 30 minutes, or until carrot and celery are tender. Season with salt and pepper.

*One cup (250 mL)...Energy 119cal/498kJ;
Fat 6.2g; Protein 12g; Carbohydrate 3g*

Two-Day Barley Soup

Prepare the beef on Day 1. Soup cooks for 1 hour on Day 2. Makes 12 cups (3 L).

3	Beef shanks, bone-in	3
10 cups	Water	2.5 L
2 tbsp.	Beef bouillon powder	30 mL
4-5	Celery stalks, with leaves	4-5
1	Small whole onion, peeled	1
2	Bay leaves	2
10	Peppercorns	10
1 tsp.	Salt	5 mL
	Freshly ground pepper, to taste	
	Reserved beef broth	
⅔ cup	Pearl barley	150 mL
3	Carrots, quartered lengthwise and sliced	3
1 cup	Chopped onion	250 mL
1 cup	Chopped celery	250 mL
2-3	Medium potatoes, diced	2-3
10 oz.	Condensed tomato soup	284 mL
	Reserved diced beef shank	

■ Day 1: Combine the first 9 ingredients in a large stock pot or Dutch oven. Bring to a boil. Skim off any foam. Cover and simmer for 2 hours or until the beef is tender and falling off the bone. Remove the shanks and dice the beef. Discard the bones. Cover and refrigerate the beef. Strain the broth into a large bowl. Cover and refrigerate until the next day. ■ Day 2: Remove the hardened fat from the surface of the beef broth and discard. Heat the broth in the stock pot until boiling. Add the barley, carrots, onion and celery. Simmer, covered, for 45 minutes or until the barley is almost cooked. Add the potatoes and continue to simmer, covered, for about 15 minutes. Stir in the tomato soup and reserved diced beef. Heat through. Remove the bay leaves.

One cup (250 mL)… Energy 147cal/613kJ; Fat 2.5g; Protein 12g; Carbohydrate 20g

Spicy Beef and Rice Soup

Eliminate the chilies for a milder flavor.
Makes 8 cups (2 L).

1 lb.	Minute steaks	454 g
2 tsp.	Vegetable oil	10 mL
1	Garlic clove, minced	1
¼ cup	Finely chopped onion	60 mL
2 tbsp.	Chopped fresh sweet basil	30 mL
½ tsp.	Dried oregano	2 mL
¼ tsp.	Dried thyme	1 mL
¼ tsp.	Crushed chilies	1 mL
½ tsp.	Salt	2 mL
⅛ tsp.	Pepper	0.5 mL
5 cups	Water	1.25 L
14 oz.	Canned diced Mexican-style tomatoes, drained	398 mL
½ cup	Long grain white rice, uncooked	125 mL
¼ tsp.	Chili powder	1 mL
	Hot pepper sauce, to taste	
2 tbsp.	Chopped fresh cilantro	30 mL

■ Cut the steaks into 1 inch (2.5 cm) strips and then across into 1 inch (2.5 cm) cubes. Heat the oil in a non-stick skillet and add the steak, garlic and onion. Sauté just until the beef changes color. Place the beef in a bowl and season with the basil, oregano, thyme, chilies, salt and pepper. Cover and let stand.

■ Combine the water, tomatoes, rice, chili powder and hot pepper sauce in a Dutch oven. Bring to a boil. Reduce the heat and cover tightly. Simmer for 20 minutes. Add the cooked beef and heat thoroughly. Gently stir in the cilantro and serve immediately.

One cup (250 mL)…Energy 157cal/657kJ;
Fat 5.4g; Protein 14g; Carbohydrate 12g

CHAPTER 10

Steaks

Zesty Broiled Steak, page 152

A Round of Draft

Start the day before. Allow about 1½ hours to barbecue and make sauce. Serves 10.

3 lbs.	Round steak, 2 inches (5 cm) thick	1.4 kg

MARINADE

12 oz.	Canned or bottled beer	355 mL
¼ cup	Vegetable oil	60 mL
2 tbsp.	Cider vinegar	30 mL
2 tbsp.	Brown sugar	30 mL
1	Medium onion, thinly sliced	1
2	Garlic cloves, minced	2
1	Bay leaf	1
½ tsp.	Ground thyme	2 mL
½ tsp.	Salt	2 mL
¼ tsp.	Freshly ground pepper	1 mL
Pinch	Brown sugar	Pinch

■ Pierce the steak in several places with a thin metal skewer or fork. Place in a shallow dish or sealable plastic bag. ■ Combine the 10 marinade ingredients and pour over the steak. Turn to coat. Cover or seal. Marinate in the refrigerator for 8 hours or overnight, turning several times. Remove the steak, reserving the marinade. ■ Barbecue over high heat for 3 to 4 minutes per side. Continue barbecuing by the indirect cooking method (see page 8) over medium heat for 20 minutes per lb. (45 minutes per kg.) or to desired doneness. Brush twice with the reserved marinade. ■ Remove the onion from the marinade. Discard the bay leaf. Sauté the onion, with the brown sugar, in a non-stick skillet until the onion is soft. Pour in the remaining marinade and boil until reduced by ⅓. ■ Cut the steak across the grain into ½ inch (12 mm) strips. Top with the onion mixture.

One serving… Energy 223cal/932kJ; Fat 8.8g; Protein 27g; Carbohydrate 5g

Sweet and Sour Steak

Ready in 15 minutes. Serve with the sauce and rice. Serves 4.

1 tsp.	Vegetable oil	5 mL
1 lb.	Eye of round or sirloin tip steak	454 g

SAUCE

½ cup	Sweet and sour barbecue sauce	125 mL
¼ cup	Mild or hot chutney	60 mL
¼ cup	Chopped onion	60 mL
1 tbsp.	Soy sauce	15 mL

■ Heat the oil in a non-stick skillet. Brown the steak quickly on both sides.
■ Combine the 4 sauce ingredients in a small bowl. Spoon over the steak. Simmer, uncovered, for 6 to 10 minutes, turning once, until the beef is no longer pink.

One serving… Energy 163cal/683kJ; Fat 4.4g; Protein 23g; Carbohydrate 7g

Pepper Steak for Two

Ready in only 10 minutes. Try with Salsa Romescu, page 15, or Béarnaise Sauce, page 12. Serves 2.

½ lb.	Round steak	225 g
1 tsp.	Freshly ground black or mixed pepper	5 mL
2 tsp.	Hard margarine	10 mL
1 tbsp.	Dry white wine	15 mL
1 tsp.	Worcestershire sauce	5 mL
1	Garlic clove, minced	1
¼ tsp.	Celery salt	1 mL

■ Cut the steak into ¼ inch (6 mm) strips. Rub the pepper into both sides of the strips with the heel of your hand. ■ Melt the margarine in a heavy skillet. Add the remaining 4 ingredients. Stir. Add the steak. Cook, stirring constantly, for about 3½ minutes, or to desired doneness.

One serving… Energy 161cal/673kJ; Fat 6.6g; Protein 22g; Carbohydrate 2g

Italian Steak

Serve with the sauce and green spinach noodles. Serves 6.

1½ lbs.	Round steak	680 g

MARINADE

½ cup	Dry white wine	125 mL
	Freshly ground pepper, to taste	
2	Sprigs fresh rosemary, chopped	2
2 tbsp.	Chopped fresh sweet basil	30 mL
1	Bay leaf	1

SAUCE

7½ oz.	Tomato sauce	213 mL
¼ cup	Chopped onion	60 mL
½ tsp.	Minced garlic	2 mL
1 tbsp.	Chopped fresh sweet basil	15 mL
½ tsp.	Dried oregano	2 mL

■ Pound the steak with a meat mallet. Place in a shallow dish or sealable plastic bag. Combine the wine, pepper, rosemary, first amount of basil and the bay leaf and pour over the steak. Turn to coat. Cover or seal. Marinate in the refrigerator overnight, turning several times. ■ Remove the steak, straining and reserving the marinade. Place on the rack in a broiler pan. Broil the steak for about 8 minutes per side for rare or to desired doneness. ■ Combine the remaining ingredients and the reserved marinade in a small saucepan and bring to a boil. Reduce the heat and cover. Simmer for 5 to 10 minutes. Slice the steak thinly across the grain. Arrange on a warmed platter.

One serving… Energy 145cal/606kJ; Fat 2.8g; Protein 22g; Carbohydrate 4g

Zesty Broiled Steak

Ready in less than 30 minutes. Serves 2.

1 tbsp.	Soy sauce	15 mL
1	Small garlic clove, crushed	1
1 tsp.	Grated orange peel	5 mL
½ tsp.	Dried rosemary, crumbled	2 mL
½ lb.	Sirloin, rib-eye or strip loin steak, ¾ inch (2 cm) thick	225 g

GARNISH

Sesame seeds	
Orange twist	

■ Combine the soy sauce, garlic, orange peel and rosemary in a small cup. Coat both sides of the beef with the mixture until used up. Let the seasoned steak stand for 10 minutes to allow the flavors to penetrate. Place on the rack in a broiler pan. Broil for 4 to 6 minutes per side or to desired doneness. ■ Sprinkle with sesame seeds and garnish with an orange twist.

One serving… Energy 151cal/631kJ;
Fat 4.9g; Protein 23g; Carbohydrate 2g

Broiled Herbed Rouladen

Ready in under 15 minutes. Double or triple recipe to suit. Serves 2.

2 tbsp.	Dijon mustard	30 mL
2	Rouladen steaks, about 4 oz. (125 g) each, or top round slices, ¼ inch (6 mm) each	2
2 tbsp.	Finely chopped fresh parsley	30 mL

■ Spread the mustard on 1 side of each steak. Sprinkle with the parsley. Roll up and hold the seam closed with toothpicks or skewers. Place on the rack in a broiler pan. Broil, seam side down, for 4 minutes. Turn and broil for 3 minutes. Do not overcook. Slice each roll into ¼ inch (6 mm) slices and fan out on each plate.

One serving… Energy 142cal/595kJ;
Fat 3.9g; Protein 25g; Carbohydrate 1g

Acapulco Beef Filet

Have two skillets going at once to save time.
Serves 4.

1 tbsp.	Hard margarine	15 mL
1	Large onion, cut lengthwise into slivers	1
1	Red pepper, cut into 1½ inch (3.8 cm) chunks	1
1	Yellow pepper, cut into 1½ inch (3.8 cm) chunks	1
3 tbsp.	Chili sauce	50 mL
½ cup	Condensed beef broth	125 mL
½ tsp.	Salt	2 mL
1 tsp.	Freshly ground pepper	5 mL
4 x 4 oz.	Filet or tenderloin steaks	4 x 125 g
	Freshly ground pepper, to taste	
1 tbsp.	Vegetable oil	15 mL
2 tbsp.	Tequila	30 mL
1 tbsp.	Lime juice	15 mL
¼ tsp.	Salt	1 mL

■ Melt the margarine in a non-stick skillet. Sauté the onion, stirring frequently, until golden. Add the red and yellow peppers and sauté for 2 to 3 minutes. Add the chili sauce, beef broth, salt and pepper. Cover and simmer for 7 minutes. ■ Blot the steaks with paper towels. Season with freshly ground pepper. Rub in well. ■ Heat the oil in a cast iron skillet until very hot. Sear the steaks for 3 to 4 minutes per side or to desired doneness. Arrange the drained vegetables on a warmed platter. Place the steaks on top. Add the tequila and lime juice to the cast iron skillet. Simmer for 2 to 3 minutes. Sprinkle with the salt. Pour the sauce over the steaks.

One serving… Energy 271cal/1135kJ;
Fat 13.7g; Protein 25g; Carbohydrate 7g

Tenderloin with Mixed Peppercorn Sauce

Tenderloin is at its best if rare or medium rare. Do not overcook. Serves 4.

4 x 4 oz.	Tenderloin steaks	4 x 125 g
1 tsp.	Crushed mixed peppercorns	5 mL
2 tsp.	Vegetable oil	10 mL
¼ cup	Condensed beef broth	60 mL
1 tbsp.	Gin	15 mL
2 tbsp.	Table cream	30 mL

■ Rub the steaks with the peppercorn. Heat the oil in a cast iron skillet until very hot. Sear the steaks for 3 to 4 minutes per side or to desired doneness. Remove the steaks and keep warm. ■ Pour the beef broth and gin into the skillet. Simmer until reduced to ½. Add the cream and simmer for 2 minutes. Serve over the steaks.

One serving… Energy 204cal/853kJ; Fat 10.2g; Protein 24g; Carbohydrate 1g

Dijon Lemon Steak

Simple and quick. Only about 20 minutes in total time. Serves 4.

SAUCE

3 tbsp.	Dijon mustard	50 mL
1½ tsp.	Lemon juice	7 mL
1 tsp.	Worcestershire sauce	5 mL
1	Large garlic clove, minced	1
½ tsp.	Freshly ground pepper	2 mL
1 lb.	Strip loin steak	454 g

■ Mix together the mustard, lemon juice, Worcestershire sauce, garlic and pepper. ■ Brush the mustard mixture on both sides of the steak. Place on the rack in a broiler pan. Broil for 5 to 6 minutes per side or to desired doneness. Brush occasionally with additional mixture, if desired.

One serving... Energy 156cal/654kJ; Fat 6.1g; Protein 23g; Carbohydrate 1g

Sesame Steak

Prepare in 5 minutes the day before. Do on the barbecue, if desired. Serves 4.

1½ lbs.	Round, cross-rib or boneless blade steak, 1 inch (2.5 cm) thick	680 g

MARINADE

1 tbsp.	Vegetable oil	15 mL
⅓ cup	Soy sauce	75 mL
¼ cup	Granulated sugar	60 mL
¼ cup	Chopped green onion	60 mL
2 tbsp.	Toasted sesame seeds	30 mL
3	Garlic cloves, minced	3
⅛ tsp.	Hot pepper sauce	0.5 mL

■ Pierce the steak several times with a fork and place in a shallow dish or sealable plastic bag. ■ Combine the 7 marinade ingredients and pour over the steak. Turn to coat. Cover or seal. Marinate in the refrigerator for at least 12 hours or overnight, turning several times. Remove the steak, discarding the marinade. Place on the rack in a broiler pan. Broil for 7 to 9 minutes per side or to desired doneness.

One serving... Energy 206/860kJ; Fat 10g; Protein 23g; Carbohydrate 4g

Teriyaki Steak

So quick and easy. 10 minutes to prepare and about 10 minutes to broil. Serves 6.

SAUCE

¼ cup	Soy sauce	60 mL
2 tbsp.	Cooking sherry	30 mL
1 tbsp.	Granulated sugar	15 mL
1	Garlic clove, minced	1
½ tsp.	Freshly grated gingerroot	2 mL
¼ tsp.	Pepper	1 mL

1½ lbs.	Rib-eye or sirloin steak, 1 inch (2.5 cm) thick	680 g

■ Combine the 6 sauce ingredients in a small saucepan. Heat and stir to dissolve the sugar. ■ Brush both sides of the steak with the sauce. Place on the rack in a broiler pan. Broil the steak for 5 to 6 minutes per side or to desired doneness. Baste with the sauce when the steaks are turned. ■ Pour any remaining sauce over the steak to serve.

One serving… Energy 164cal/688kJ; Fat 6g; Protein 22g; Carbohydrate 3g

Steak Rubs

Double or triple your favorite rub and keep a quantity handy in a closed container for a quick tasty steaks or burgers.

LEMON PEPPER RUB

1 tsp.	Dried lemon peel	5 mL
1 tsp.	Garlic powder	5 mL
1 tsp.	Lemon pepper	5 mL
½ tsp.	Dried sweet basil	2 mL

One recipe... Energy 19cal/81kJ;
Fat trace; Protein 1g; Carbohydrate 5g

HERB AND SPICE RUB

1 tbsp.	Dried parsley, crumbled	15 mL
1 tsp.	Paprika	5 mL
1 tsp.	Garlic powder	5 mL
¼ tsp.	Pepper	1 mL

One recipe... Energy 18cal/75kJ;
Fat 0.4g; Protein 1g; Carbohydrate 4g

CHILI RUB

1 tsp.	Onion powder	5 mL
1 tsp.	Chili powder	5 mL
1 tsp.	Garlic salt	5 mL
1 tsp.	Dried oregano, crushed	5 mL
1 tsp.	Ground cumin	5 mL

One recipe... Energy 38cal/159kJ;
Fat 1.1g; Protein 2g; Carbohydrate 7g

NEW ORLEANS RUB

1 tsp.	Garlic salt	5 mL
1 tsp.	Curry powder	5 mL
1 tsp.	Paprika	5 mL
¼ tsp.	Cayenne pepper	1 mL

One recipe... Energy 19cal/79kJ;
Fat 0.6g; Protein 1g; Carbohydrate 4g

■ Combine the ingredients of one of the above rubs in a small cup. Rub on both sides of steaks, using the heel of your hand, or sprinkle on burgers. Use as little or as much rub as desired. ■ Broil or grill the steaks or burgers to desired doneness.

Stews

Curried Beef Stew, page 164

Beef Bourguignonne

Prepare the onions the day before or in the morning. Keep in cold water after peeling. Serves 6.

¼ cup	All-purpose flour	60 mL
¼ tsp.	Salt	1 mL
¼ tsp.	Pepper	1 mL
2 lbs.	Round, blade or sirloin steak, cut into ¾ inch (2 cm) cubes	900 g
2 cups	Dry red wine	500 mL
10 oz.	Condensed beef consommé	284 mL
2	Bay leaves	2
1½ tsp.	Vegetable oil	7 mL
1	Garlic clove, minced	1
2 cups	Sliced fresh mushrooms	500 mL
	Freshly ground pepper, to taste	
2	Baskets pearl onions	2
3½ cups	Diagonally sliced carrot	875 mL
¼ cup	Chopped fresh parsley	60 mL

■ Combine the flour, salt and pepper in a plastic bag. Add the beef cubes, a few at a time, and shake to coat. Place the beef cubes in a lightly sprayed roaster. Bake, uncovered, in a 425°F (220°C) oven for 10 minutes or until browned, stirring once. Add the wine, consommé and bay leaves. Lower the temperature to 350°F (175°C). Cover and bake for 2 to 2½ hours. ■ Heat the oil in a non-stick skillet. Sauté the garlic, mushrooms and pepper until browned. Add to the beef mixture. ■ Pour boiling water over the onions to loosen the skins. Drain and rinse in cold water. Cut off the ends and peel the onions. Add the onions, carrot and parsley to the beef. Stir. Cover and cook for 1 hour or until the beef and vegetables are tender. Remove the bay leaves. ■ Serve over hot cooked noodles.

One serving… Energy 288cal/1206kJ; Fat 7g; Protein 33g; Carbohydrate 16g

Hearty Beef Stew

Prepare the vegetables while the beef is browning.
Allow 1½ hours all together. Serves 8.

¼ cup	All-purpose flour	60 mL
1 tsp.	Salt	5 mL
¼ tsp.	Pepper	1 mL
2 lbs.	Stewing beef	900 g
1 cup	Water	250 mL
½ cup	Ketchup	125 mL
¼ cup	Brown sugar, packed	60 mL
¼ cup	White vinegar	60 mL
1 tbsp.	Worcestershire sauce	15 mL
1 tsp.	Salt	5 mL
1	Large onion, chopped	1
½	Medium green pepper, cut into strips	½
3	Medium carrots, cut into ¾ inch (2 cm) pieces	3
3	Medium potatoes, cut into chunks	3

■ Combine the flour, salt and pepper in a plastic bag. Add the beef cubes, a few at a time, and shake to coat. Place the beef cubes in a lightly sprayed roaster. Bake, uncovered, in a 350°F (175°C) oven for 20 minutes or until browned. Remove the beef to a Dutch oven. ■ Combine the water, ketchup, brown sugar, vinegar, Worcestershire sauce and salt. Stir into the browned beef. Add the onion. Cover and simmer for 40 minutes, stirring occasionally. ■ Add the remaining vegetables. Cover and simmer for 30 minutes or until the beef and vegetables are tender.

One serving… Energy 222cal/929kJ;
Fat 3.6g; Protein 20g; Carbohydrate 28g

Stout Beef Stew

Stew can be cooled after the first baking and refrigerated overnight. Finish baking at the reduced temperature. Serves 6.

½ cup	All-purpose flour	125 mL
1 tsp.	Seasoned salt	5 mL
	Freshly ground pepper, to taste	
2 lbs.	Stewing beef	900 g
1 tbsp.	Hard margarine	15 mL
1 tbsp.	Vegetable oil	15 mL
2	Medium onions, thinly sliced in rings	2
2	Garlic cloves, crushed	2
2 cups	Sliced fresh mushrooms	500 mL
	Reserved seasoned flour	
5½ oz.	Tomato paste	156 mL
1⅓ cups	Stout beer	325 mL
2 cups	Water	500 mL
1 tsp.	White vinegar	5 mL
3	Bay leaves	3
	Salt, to taste	

■ Combine the flour, seasoned salt and pepper in a plastic bag. Add the beef cubes, a few at a time, and shake to coat. Reserve any leftover flour. ■ Spread the beef cubes on a lightly sprayed baking sheet. Lightly spray the beef as well. ■ Broil, turning the beef several times, until browned. ■ Heat the margarine and oil in a Dutch oven. Sauté the onion, garlic and mushrooms for 10 minutes. Add the reserved flour, tomato paste, beer, water, vinegar and bay leaves. Stir and bring to a boil. Season with salt. Add the browned beef. Cover and bake in a 325°F (160°C) oven for 1 hour. ■ Reduce the temperature to 300°F (150°C) and cook for 1½ hours or until the beef is tender. Discard the bay leaves.

One serving... Energy 291cal/1216kJ;
Fat 9.3g; Protein 27g; Carbohydrate 21g

Yorkshire Stew

The stew can be made the day before. Ready in less than 1 hour on serving day. Serves 6.

STEW

2 lbs.	Bottom round steak, trimmed of fat, cut into 1 inch (2.5 cm) cubes	900 g
¼ cup	All-purpose flour	60 mL
2 tsp.	Vegetable oil	10 mL
1	Medium onion, thinly sliced	1
6	Medium fresh mushrooms, sliced	6
10 oz.	Condensed beef broth	284 mL
½ cup	Dry red wine	125 mL
½ tsp.	Salt	2 mL
¼ tsp.	Pepper	1 mL
¼ tsp.	Dried rosemary, crushed	1 mL
¼ tsp.	Dried tarragon	1 mL
1 tbsp.	Tomato paste	15 mL
1 tsp.	Worcestershire sauce	5 mL
3	Medium carrots, cut into 1 inch (2.5 cm) pieces	3

YORKSHIRE PUDDING

2	Large eggs	2
1 cup	1% milk	250 mL
1 cup	All-purpose flour	250 mL
½ tsp.	Salt	2 mL
2 tbsp.	Hard margarine	30 mL

■ Toss the beef cubes with the flour in a plastic bag. ■ Brown the beef cubes on a lightly sprayed baking sheet in a 425°F (220°C) oven for about 10 minutes, stirring once. ■ Heat the oil in a Dutch oven. Add the onion and sauté until soft. Stir in the mushrooms and sauté for 3 to 4 minutes. ■ Add the broth, wine, salt, pepper, rosemary, tarragon, tomato paste and Worcestershire sauce. Stir well. Add the beef. Cover and simmer for 1 hour. ■ Add the carrot and cook for 1 hour or until the beef is tender. ■ Beat the eggs in a medium bowl until frothy. Stir in the milk. Blend well. Combine the flour and salt in a small bowl. Beat into the milk mixture until smooth. ■ Place the margarine in an ungreased 2 quart (2 L) casserole dish. Heat in a 400°F (205°C) oven for 3 minutes or until melted. Remove the dish from the oven and immediately pour the batter in. Using a slotted spoon, carefully place the stew in center of the batter to within 1 inch (2.5 cm) of the edge, reserving the gravy. Return the dish to the oven and bake, uncovered, for 30 minutes. Reheat the gravy and slowly pour over the hot stew. Serve immediately.

One serving… Energy 419cal/1753kJ; Fat 13.9g; Protein 37g; Carbohydrate 31g

Curried Beef Stew

The flavor is best if made the day before. Bring to room temperature and reheat, covered, for 20 minutes until heated through. Serves 4.

1	Medium apple, diced	1
1	Small onion, thinly sliced	1
2 tsp.	Vegetable oil	10 mL
1½ tsp.	Curry powder	7 mL
2 tsp.	Granulated sugar	10 mL
1 tsp.	Ground cumin	5 mL
1 lb.	Stewing beef	454 g
19 oz.	Canned tomatoes, with juice, chopped	540 mL
1 tbsp.	Lemon juice	15 mL
1 tsp.	Beef bouillon powder	5 mL
¼ cup	Hot water	60 mL
⅓ cup	Raisins	75 mL
½ tsp.	Freshly grated gingerroot	2 mL
¾ tsp.	Salt	4 mL
¼ tsp.	Pepper	1 mL
⅓ cup	Diced green pepper	75 mL
1 tbsp.	Cornstarch	15 mL
2 tbsp.	Cold water	30 mL

■ Sauté the apple and onion in the oil in a large non-stick skillet for about 3 minutes. Add the curry, sugar and cumin and mix well. Remove the mixture to a small bowl. ■ Brown the beef cubes in the skillet. Return the apple and onion mixture to the skillet. ■ Add the next 8 ingredients and stir well. Cover and simmer for 45 minutes. ■ Add the green pepper. Simmer for 10 minutes or until the beef is tender. Adjust the seasoning to taste. ■ Combine the cornstarch and water in a small cup. Stir into the stew to thicken.

One serving… Energy 242cal/1013kJ;
Fat 6.6g; Protein 20g; Carbohydrate 28g

Pasta and Stew

Allow 3 hours to prepare and cook. Serves 6.

3 tbsp.	All-purpose flour	50 mL
1 tsp.	Paprika	5 mL
1 tsp.	Salt	5 mL
¼ tsp.	Freshly ground pepper	1 mL
1½ lbs.	Round or blade steak, cut into 1 inch (2.5 cm) cubes	680 g
2 tbsp.	Olive oil	30 mL
1	Garlic clove, minced	1
1	Medium onion, cut into large chunks	1
1 tbsp.	Chopped fresh thyme	15 mL
1 tsp.	Olive oil	5 mL
14 oz.	Canned tomatoes, with juice, mashed	398 mL
¼ cup	Barbecue sauce	60 mL
2 x 10 oz.	Condensed beef broth	2 x 284 mL
1	Bay leaf	1
4	Carrots, sliced coin size	4
1	Celery stalk, sliced	1
2 cups	Sliced fresh mushrooms	500 mL
1½ cups	Wagon wheel pasta, uncooked	375 mL

■ Combine the flour, paprika, salt and pepper in a plastic bag. Add the beef cubes, a few at a time, and shake to coat. Heat the first amount of oil in a Dutch oven. Brown the beef cubes on all sides. Remove to a bowl. ■ Sauté the garlic, onion and thyme in the second amount of oil until the onion is just soft. Add the next 4 ingredients. Stir to mix well. Add the reserved beef cubes and bring to a boil. Cover and simmer for 1½ hours. ■ Add the carrots. Cover and simmer for 30 minutes. Add the celery, mushrooms and pasta. Cover and simmer for 20 minutes or until the vegetables and pasta are cooked. Discard the bay leaf before serving.

One serving… Energy 364cal/1523kJ;
Fat 10.7g; Protein 32g; Carbohydrate 35g

Hungarian Stew

Regular paprika can be used instead of the Hungarian but with less flavorful results. Serves 6.

¼ cup	All-purpose flour	60 mL
2 tsp.	Hungarian paprika	10 mL
¼ tsp.	Salt	1 mL
½ tsp.	Freshly ground pepper	2 mL
1½ lbs.	Round, sirloin or blade steak, cut into ¾ inch (2 cm) cubes	680 g
2 tsp.	Vegetable oil	10 mL
1	Large onion, thinly sliced	1
2	Garlic cloves, minced	2
1	Large red pepper, cut in slivers	1
⅛ tsp.	Caraway seed	0.5 mL
1½ cups	Condensed beef broth	375 mL
2 tbsp.	Tomato paste	30 mL
2 tsp.	Hungarian paprika	10 mL
2 cups	Sliced carrot, cut coin size	500 mL
1 cup	Non-fat sour cream	250 mL

■ Combine the flour, paprika, salt and pepper in a plastic bag. Add the beef cubes, a few at a time, and shake to coat. Place the beef cubes in a lightly sprayed roaster. Bake, uncovered, in a 425°F (220°C) oven for 10 minutes or until browned, stirring once. Remove the beef to a bowl. ■ Heat the oil in a Dutch oven and stir-fry the next 4 ingredients for 5 minutes. Add the beef. Stir in the next 4 ingredients and bring to a boil. Cover and simmer for 1 hour or until the beef is tender. ■ Remove from the heat and gently stir in the sour cream.

One serving… Energy 230cal/959kJ; Fat 6.1g; Protein 27g; Carbohydrate 17g

Porcupine Meatball Stew

Allow 2½ hours in total but preparation is only 30 minutes. Serves 6.

1½ lbs.	Lean ground beef	680 g
½ cup	Long grain white rice, uncooked	125 mL
1	Garlic clove, crushed	1
1 tsp.	Salt	5 mL
½ tsp.	Pepper	2 mL
⅓ cup	Dry bread crumbs	75 mL
1	Large egg, fork-beaten	1
½ cup	Finely chopped onion	125 mL
3 cups	Tomato juice	750 mL
2 tbsp.	All-purpose flour	30 mL
1 tbsp.	Brown sugar, packed	15 mL
½ tsp.	Salt	2 mL
½ tsp.	Pepper	2 mL
6	Medium carrots, thinly sliced coin size	6
4	Medium potatoes, cut into 6 pieces each	4
1	Small onion, quartered	1
1	Bay leaf	1

■ Combine the beef with the next 7 ingredients in a medium bowl. Form into 1½ inch (3.8 cm) balls. Place in a lightly sprayed medium roaster. Bake in a 350°F (175°C) oven for 20 minutes.

■ Combine the tomato juice with the flour, brown sugar, salt and pepper and pour ½ the juice mixture over the meatballs. Add the carrot, potato, onion and bay leaf. Stir gently. Pour the remaining juice mixture over all.

■ Cover and bake in a 350°F (175°C) oven for 2 hours or until the rice is cooked and the vegetables are tender. Discard the bay leaf.

One serving… Energy 439cal/1836kJ;
Fat 18.6g; Protein 27g; Carbohydrate 41g

CHAPTER 12

Stir-Frys

Spicy Beef with Asparagus, page 178

Penne with Tomato and Beef

Prepare the vegetables while the pasta is cooking. Serves 6.

2 cups	Penne or rigatoni pasta, uncooked	500 mL
1 lb.	Top round steak, cut into ⅛ inch (3 mm) strips	454 g
2	Garlic cloves, minced	2
2 tbsp.	Finely chopped onion	30 mL
2 tbsp.	Chopped fresh sweet basil	30 mL
1 tsp.	Dried thyme	5 mL
1 tsp.	Dried oregano	5 mL
5½ oz.	Tomato paste	156 mL
19 oz.	Canned tomatoes, with juice, puréed	540 mL
1	Medium green pepper, cut into thin strips	1

GARNISH

Freshly ground pepper
Freshly grated mozzarella cheese

■ Cook the pasta according to package directions. Drain and cover with cold water. ■ Heat a non-stick skillet or wok until hot. Stir-fry the beef strips for 1 to 2 minutes. Add the garlic, onion and herbs. Stir-fry for 2 minutes or until the beef is no longer pink. Push the beef mixture to one side and stir in the tomato paste and puréed tomato. Mix well. Cover and simmer for 15 minutes. Add the green pepper. Continue to simmer, covered, for about 5 minutes or until the beef is tender. ■ Drain the pasta and add to the beef mixture. Stir until heated through. ■ Garnish with pepper and mozzarella cheese.

One serving… Energy 269cal/1127kJ;
Fat 3.7g; Protein 22g; Carbohydrate 39g

Three Pepper Stir-Fry

Prepare the vegetables in the morning. Prepare the beef and marinate ahead of time. Serves 4.

1 lb.	Top round or sirloin steak	454 g
2	Garlic cloves, minced	2
2 tbsp.	Oyster sauce	30 mL
1 tbsp.	Vegetable oil	15 mL
1 tsp.	Vegetable oil	5 mL
1 tsp.	Sesame oil	5 mL
1	Medium green pepper, sliced diagonally into 1 x 2 inch (2.5 x 5 cm) chunks	1
1	Medium red pepper, sliced diagonally into 1 x 2 inch (2.5 x 5 cm) chunks	1
1	Medium yellow pepper, sliced diagonally into 1 x 2 inch (2.5 x 5 cm) chunks	1
1	Medium onion, cut into slivers	1
2	Large celery stalks, cut into thin diagonal slices	2
1 tsp.	Beef bouillon powder	5 mL
½ cup	Boiling water	125 mL
1 tbsp.	Soy sauce	15 mL
1 tsp.	Brown sugar	5 mL
¼ tsp.	Crushed chilies	1 mL
2 tsp.	Cornstarch	10 mL

■ Trim all visible fat from the beef. Cut the beef lengthwise into 2 inch (5 cm) strips. Cut the strips crosswise into ¼ inch (6 mm) slices. Julienne the strips lengthwise into thin strips. ■ Combine the garlic and oyster sauce with the beef and marinate for 1 hour. ■ Heat the first amount of vegetable oil in a non-stick skillet or wok until hot. Add the beef with the marinade. Stir-fry, uncovered, for 3 minutes or until the beef is no longer pink. Remove the beef with a slotted spoon to a small bowl. Pour off the liquid and wipe out the skillet. ■ Add the second amount of vegetable oil and the sesame oil to the skillet. Heat until hot. Add all the vegetables. Toss and stir-fry for 3 to 5 minutes. Add the beef. ■ Combine the bouillon powder and water with the remaining 4 ingredients in a small cup. Pour into the center of the wok. Stir until bubbling and thickened.

One serving… Energy 228cal/956kJ; Fat 9.2g; Protein 24g; Carbohydrate 12g

Thai Beef and Pasta

Ready in 30 minutes. Serve immediately. Serves 4.

4 oz.	Vermicelli or capellini pasta, broken in half, uncooked	125 g
1½ tsp.	Sesame oil	7 mL
1 lb.	Sirloin steak, cut across the grain into thin strips, or beef stir-fry strips	454 g
4	Garlic cloves, minced	4
3	Jalapeño peppers, seeded and finely chopped (wear gloves)	3
3 tbsp.	Oyster sauce	50 mL
1 tsp.	Granulated sugar	5 mL
1 tsp.	Lemon pepper	5 mL
1 tbsp.	Vegetable oil	15 mL
¼ cup	Chopped fresh sweet basil	60 mL
1 tbsp.	Chopped fresh mint	15 mL
1 tbsp.	Coarsely chopped roasted salted peanuts	15 mL

GARNISH

Lemon slices

■ Cook the pasta according to package directions. Drain. Toss with the sesame oil. Keep warm. ■ Combine the beef strips with the garlic, jalapeño pepper, oyster sauce, sugar, lemon pepper and oil. Mix together well. Heat a non-stick skillet or wok until hot. Stir-fry the beef strip mixture for 5 to 6 minutes or until the beef is no longer pink. Pour over the pasta. Sprinkle with the basil, mint and roasted peanuts. ■ Garnish with lemon slices.

One serving… Energy 343cal/1434kJ; Fat 11.2g; Protein 28g; Carbohydrate 32g

Beef and Celery in Oyster Sauce

Serve over rice as there is lots of sauce. Serves 4.

¼ cup	Soy sauce	60 mL
2 tbsp.	Sherry or apple juice	30 mL
1 tsp.	Granulated sugar	5 mL
¼ tsp.	Sesame oil	1 mL
1 tbsp.	Cornstarch	15 mL
1 lb.	Flank, round or blade steak, cut thinly across the grain	454 g
2 tsp.	Cornstarch	10 mL
¼ cup	Water	60 mL
⅓ cup	Oyster sauce	75 mL
1 tsp.	Vegetable oil	5 mL
1	Medium onion, cut into slivers	1
3 cups	Sliced celery, cut on the diagonal	750 mL
2 tsp.	Vegetable oil	10 mL
1 tbsp.	Freshly grated gingerroot	15 mL

■ Combine the soy sauce, sherry, sugar, sesame oil and first amount of cornstarch in a small bowl. Add the beef strips and marinate for at least 10 minutes.

■ Combine the second amount of cornstarch with the water and oyster sauce in a small cup. ■ Heat the first amount of vegetable oil in a non-stick skillet or wok until hot. Stir-fry the onion and celery for 4 minutes. Remove to a bowl. ■ Heat the second amount of vegetable oil in the same skillet until hot. Add the ginger. Stir-fry for a few seconds. Add the beef strips with the marinade and stir-fry until the beef is no longer pink. Add the oyster sauce mixture and heat to thicken. Add the onion and celery and stir to heat through.

One serving… Energy 291cal/1216kJ;
Fat 12.5g; Protein 28g; Carbohydrate 14g

Spaghetti Stir-Fry

Only 15 minutes from start to finish! Serves 6.

12 oz.	Whole wheat or regular spaghetti pasta, uncooked	375 g
3 cups	Frozen Oriental or Italian mixed vegetables	750 mL
1 lb.	Round or sirloin tip steak, cut into thin slices	454 g
⅔ cup	Chili sauce	150 mL
2 tbsp.	Water	30 mL

■ Cook the spaghetti according to package directions, adding the frozen vegetables during the last 5 minutes of cooking time. ■ Heat a non-stick skillet or wok until hot. Stir-fry the beef for about 4 minutes or until no longer pink. Add the chili sauce and water. Stir to heat through. Toss the drained spaghetti and vegetable mixture with the beef.

One serving… Energy 233cal/975kJ; Fat 3.8g; Protein 22g; Carbohydrate 31g

Beef and Bok Choy with Black Bean Sauce

Ready in 30 minutes. Serves 4.

1 lb.	Top round or flank steak	454 g
1 tbsp.	Cornstarch	15 mL
2 tbsp.	Soy sauce	30 mL
¼ cup	Black bean sauce	60 mL
2 tbsp.	Sherry	30 mL
2 tsp.	Vegetable oil	10 mL
1	Garlic clove, minced	1
1	Small onion, sliced lengthwise into slivers	1
1 cup	Sliced celery, cut on the diagonal	250 mL
1 cup	Frozen peas, thawed	250 mL
3 cups	Coarsely chopped bok choy	750 mL
1 tbsp.	Vegetable oil	15 mL

■ Slice the beef very thinly across the grain. Cut into bite size strips. Set aside. ■ Combine the cornstarch, soy sauce, black bean sauce and sherry. Mix well. Set aside. ■ Heat the first amount of oil in a non-stick skillet or wok until hot. Stir-fry the garlic, onion and celery for 1 to 2 minutes. Add the peas and stir-fry 1 minute. Remove the vegetables to a bowl. Add the bok choy. Stir-fry 1 to 2 minutes. Remove to the bowl of vegetables. ■ Add the second amount of oil and stir-fry the beef strips in 2 batches for 2 to 3 minutes each. ■ Return all the beef to the skillet and add the stirred cornstarch and black bean mixture. Heat and stir until bubbling and thickened. ■ Add all the vegetables. Cover and simmer for 2 minutes to heat through.

One serving… Energy 320cal/1339kJ;
Fat 15.1g; Protein 30g; Carbohydrate 15g

Ginger Beef

Ready in 30 minutes. Flavors enhanced the next day. Serves 4.

1½ tsp.	Vegetable oil	7 mL
2	Large celery stalks, sliced diagonally into ½ inch (12 mm) pieces	2
1	Medium green pepper, thinly sliced	1
1	Medium onion, chopped	1
1½ cups	Sliced fresh mushrooms	375 mL
2	Medium carrots, cut julienne	2
1 lb.	Flank steak, thinly sliced	454 g
¼ cup	Water	60 mL
2 tbsp.	Soy sauce	30 mL
2 tsp.	Freshly grated gingerroot	10 mL
1	Garlic clove, minced	1
2 tsp.	Cornstarch	10 mL
1 tbsp.	Water	15 mL

■ Heat the oil in a non-stick skillet or wok until hot. Stir-fry the vegetables for 3 minutes. Remove the vegetables from the skillet using a slotted spoon. Stir-fry the beef in the skillet for 2 minutes or until no longer pink. Drain.
■ Add the first amount of water, soy sauce, ginger and garlic. Cover and simmer for 5 minutes or until the beef is tender. Add the vegetables. ■ Combine the cornstarch with the second amount of water and stir into the beef mixture. Heat, stirring constantly, until thickened.

One serving… Energy 252cal/1056kJ;
Fat 10.2g; Protein 28g; Carbohydrate 12g

Szechaun Beef

The gingerroot can be chopped or grated. Allow 35 minutes to prepare and cook. Serves 4.

1 lb.	Top round or sirloin steak	454 g

MARINADE

2 tbsp.	Finely chopped gingerroot	30 mL
2	Garlic cloves, crushed	2
½ tsp.	Chinese five-spice powder	2 mL
¼ tsp.	Crushed chilies	1 mL
3 tbsp.	Soy sauce	50 mL
3 tbsp.	Sherry	50 mL
1 tbsp.	Vegetable oil	15 mL

1 tsp.	Vegetable oil	5 mL
2 cups	Julienned carrots	500 mL
1 cup	Julienned celery	250 mL
8	Green onions, cut in 2 inch (5 cm) lengths and quartered lengthwise	8
2 tsp.	Cornstarch	10 mL
2 tsp.	Cold water	10 mL

■ Cut the beef into ¼ inch (6 mm) slices across the grain and then cut each strip into 2 inch (5 cm) strips. ■ Combine the 7 marinade ingredients in a jar. Cover and shake well. Pour the marinade over the beef strips. Marinate for 1 hour at room temperature. ■ Heat the second amount of oil in a non-stick skillet or wok until hot. Stir-fry the carrot, celery and green onion for 4 minutes or until just tender-crisp. Add the beef with the marinade. Stir-fry for 3 minutes or until the beef is no longer pink. ■ Stir the cornstarch and water together and add to the beef mixture, stirring until thickened.

One serving… Energy 241cal/1007kJ; Fat 9g; Protein 25g; Carbohydrate 13g

Beef Vegetable Dinner

Prepare the beef and vegetables in the morning to save time. Lots of sauce! Serves 8.

2 tbsp.	Vegetable oil	30 mL
2 lbs.	Sirloin steak, cut across the grain into ¼ x 2 inch (0.6 x 5 cm) strips	900 g
2	Garlic cloves, crushed	2
1 tbsp.	Freshly grated gingerroot	15 mL
3 cups	Thinly sliced celery, cut on the diagonal	750 mL
2	Large green peppers, cut into strips	2
1	Large onion, cut into wedges	1

SAUCE

10 oz.	Condensed beef broth	284 mL
14 oz.	Canned straw mushrooms, with liquid	398 mL
8 oz.	Canned sliced water chestnuts, drained	227 mL
6 oz.	Fresh or frozen pea pods	170 g
2 cups	Water	500 mL
2 tbsp.	Soy sauce	30 mL
2 tbsp.	Mild molasses	30 mL
1 tsp.	Salt	5 mL
1 tbsp.	Brown sugar, packed	15 mL
½ cup	Cornstarch	125 mL

■ Heat the oil in a large non-stick skillet or wok until hot. Stir-fry the beef strips, ½ at a time, for 5 minutes or until no longer pink. Remove to a Dutch oven. ■ Add the garlic, ginger, celery, green pepper and onion. Stir-fry for 5 minutes. Remove to the Dutch oven. ■ Combine the 10 sauce ingredients in the skillet and heat until bubbling. This may have to be done in 2 batches. Pour over the beef and vegetables in the Dutch oven. Stir and heat through.

One serving… Energy 270cal/1131kJ;
Fat 7.9g; Protein 26g; Carbohydrate 23g

Spicy Beef with Asparagus

Marinate beef and steam asparagus in the morning. Only 10 minutes to cook. Serves 2.

1 tbsp.	Soy sauce	15 mL
1 tbsp.	Sesame oil	15 mL
1 tbsp.	Red wine vinegar	15 mL
¼ tsp.	Crushed chilies	1 mL
1	Garlic clove, minced	1
½ lb.	Sirloin beef strips, ⅛ inch (3 mm) thick	225 g
½ lb.	Fresh asparagus, cut diagonally into 1½ inch (3.8 cm) pieces	225 g
1 tsp.	Beef bouillon powder	5 mL
2 tsp.	Cornstarch	10 mL
½ cup	Boiling water	125 mL

GARNISH

Toasted sesame seeds

■ Mix the first 5 ingredients together in a medium bowl. Add the beef strips and marinate for at least 1 hour. ■ Cook or steam the asparagus in a saucepan with water for about 8 minutes or until tender-crisp. ■ Heat a non-stick skillet or wok until hot. Remove the beef, reserving the marinade. Stir-fry for about 3 minutes or until no longer pink. ■ Mix the bouillon powder, cornstarch and water with the reserved marinade. Add to the beef. Stir until thickened. Add the asparagus. Stir to heat through. ■ Garnish with toasted sesame seeds.

One serving... Energy 251cal/1051kJ; Fat 12.2g; Protein 27g; Carbohydrate 9g

Stir-Fry Pasta and Beef

Allow 30 minutes for preparation and only 5 minutes to cook. Serves 6.

12 oz.	Vermicelli, capellini or spaghettini pasta, broken in half, uncooked	375 g
2 tsp.	Beef bouillon powder	10 mL
1 cup	Boiling water	250 mL
1 tbsp.	Freshly grated gingerroot	15 mL
1	Garlic clove, crushed	1
3 tbsp.	Soy sauce	50 mL
1 tbsp.	Cornstarch	15 mL
1 tsp.	Sesame oil	5 mL
1 lb.	Sirloin steak, cut into thin strips	454 g
3	Medium carrots, thinly sliced coin size	3
1 cup	Sliced onion	250 mL
2 cups	Broccoli florets	500 mL
1 cup	Sliced mushrooms	250 mL
1½ cups	Fresh pea pods	375 mL
2 cups	Fresh bean sprouts	500 mL
	Pepper, to taste	

■ Cook the pasta according to package directions. Drain and cover with cold water. ■ Combine the next 6 ingredients. Set aside. ■ Heat the oil in a non-stick skillet or wok until hot. Add the steak strips and carrot and stir-fry for 2 minutes or until the beef is no longer pink. ■ Add the next 4 vegetables and the broth mixture. Stir-fry for about 2 minutes. ■ Drain the pasta and add to the beef mixture. Add the bean sprouts. Season with pepper. Stir until heated through.

One serving… Energy 413cal/1505kJ; Fat 4.8g; Protein 26g; Carbohydrate 53g

Pineapple Beef Stir-Fry

Serve with hot cooked rice or broad noodles.
Serves 6.

1 lb.	Flank steak	454 g
1 tbsp.	Vegetable oil	15 mL
1	Medium onion, sliced lengthwise into 1 inch (2.5 cm) wedges	1
14 oz.	Canned pineapple chunks, with juice	398 mL
¼ cup	Brown sugar, packed	60 mL
¼ cup	White vinegar	60 mL
2 tbsp.	Chili sauce	30 mL
1 tbsp.	Soy sauce	15 mL
2 tbsp.	Cornstarch	30 mL
2 tbsp.	Cold water	30 mL
1	Medium red pepper, cut into 1 inch (2.5 cm) chunks	1
2	Medium tomatoes, cut into 8 wedges each	2

■ Cut the beef with the grain into 2 inch (5 cm) strips and then cut the strips across the grain into ⅛ inch (3 mm) slices. ■ Heat the oil in a non-stick skillet or wok until hot. Add the beef and onion and stir-fry for 3 minutes or until the beef is no longer pink.
■ Stir in the pineapple with the juice, brown sugar, vinegar, chili sauce and soy sauce. Heat to boiling. Reduce the heat. Cover and simmer for 10 minutes. ■ Combine the cornstarch and water. Stir into the beef mixture. Add the red pepper and tomato wedges. Stir-fry for 1 to 2 minutes.

One serving… Energy 252cal/1055kJ;
Fat 8.1g; Protein 18g; Carbohydrate 28g

Beef and Greens Stir-Fry

Get veggies ready in the morning. Cooks in 10 minutes. Serves 4.

1 lb.	Sirloin steak, cut into thin strips	454 g
1	Garlic clove, minced	1
2 tsp.	Freshly grated gingerroot	10 mL
1 tbsp.	Soy sauce	15 mL
1	Large onion, sliced lengthwise into 1 inch (2.5 cm) wedges	1
3 cups	Sliced fresh mushrooms	750 mL
3 cups	Broccoli florets	750 mL
1 tsp.	Chicken bouillon powder	5 mL
2 tsp.	Cornstarch	10 mL
½ cup	Water	125 mL
4	Green onions, sliced diagonally, into 1 inch (2.5 cm) pieces	4
Pinch	Chinese five-spice powder	Pinch

■ Heat a non-stick skillet or wok until hot. Combine the beef strips with the garlic, ginger, and soy sauce. Stir-fry for 2 minutes or until beef is no longer pink. ■ Add the next 3 ingredients and stir-fry for 4 minutes or until the broccoli is tender-crisp. ■ Combine the bouillon powder, cornstarch and water and stir into the beef mixture. ■ Add the green onion and five-spice powder. Stir-fry for 2 to 3 minutes or until thickened.

One serving… Energy 187cal/781kJ;
Fat 4.7g; Protein 26g; Carbohydrate 11g

Indian-Spiced Beef

Using leftover cooked beef saves time. Ready in 20 minutes. Serves 4.

1 tbsp.	Vegetable oil	15 mL
1 tbsp.	Finely chopped gingerroot	15 mL
2	Garlic cloves, minced	2
1	Medium onion, coarsely chopped	1
1 tsp.	Ground cumin	5 mL
2 cups	Cooked lean beef, cut into 2 x ¼ inch (5 x 0.6 cm) slices	500 mL
½	Medium red pepper, cut into 1 inch (2.5 cm) chunks	½
½	Medium yellow pepper, cut into 1 inch (2.5 cm) chunks	½
1	Mango, diced	1
½ tsp.	Crushed chilies	2 mL
1	Medium tomato, chopped	1
¼ tsp.	Ground cardamom	1 mL
¼ tsp.	Salt	1 mL

■ Heat the oil in a non-stick skillet or wok until hot. Add the ginger, garlic, onion and cumin. Stir-fry for 2 minutes. Add the beef. Stir-fry for 1 minute. Add the peppers, mango, chilies, tomato, cardamom and salt. Stir-fry for 2 minutes or until just heated through. Serve immediately.

One serving… Energy 219cal/914kJ;
Fat 7.9g; Protein 22g; Carbohydrate 15g

Spicy Beef and Broccoli

Preparation time 25 minutes. Cooking time 15 minutes. Serves 4.

1 lb.	Top round or flank steak	454 g
1	Egg white (large), fork-beaten	1
1 tbsp.	Cornstarch	15 mL
1 tsp.	Sherry	5 mL
½ tsp.	Salt	2 mL
½ tsp.	Pepper	2 mL
½ tsp.	Hot pepper sauce	2 mL
1 tbsp.	Soy sauce	15 mL
1 tbsp.	Chili sauce	15 mL
1 tsp.	Red wine vinegar	5 mL
1 tsp.	Granulated sugar	5 mL
1 tbsp.	Vegetable oil	15 mL
2	Garlic cloves, minced	2
1½ cups	Sliced broccoli stems, cut diagonally very thin	375 mL
1½ cups	Broccoli florets, sliced lengthwise	375 mL
1 cup	Sliced fresh mushrooms	250 mL
4	Green onions, thinly sliced	4
1 tbsp.	Vegetable oil	15 mL

■ Slice the beef very thinly across the grain. Combine the egg white, cornstarch, sherry, salt, pepper and hot pepper sauce in a medium bowl. Mix well. Add the beef strips. Marinate for at least 10 minutes.

■ Combine the soy sauce, chili sauce, vinegar and sugar in a small bowl. Mix well. Set aside. ■ Heat the first amount of oil in a non-stick skillet or wok until hot. Stir-fry the garlic and broccoli stems for 1 to 2 minutes. Add the broccoli florets, mushrooms and green onion. Stir-fry for 4 to 6 minutes or until the broccoli is bright green and tender-crisp. Remove the vegetables to a bowl. ■ Heat the second amount of the oil in the same skillet until hot. Stir-fry the beef with the marinade in 2 batches for 2 to 3 minutes each. Return all the beef to the skillet and add the chili sauce mixture. Heat and stir until bubbling. Stir in the vegetables. Cover and simmer until heated through.

One serving… Energy 293cal/1227kJ; Fat 15.5g; Protein 29g; Carbohydrate 9g

Beef with Zucchini Stir-Fry

Marinate the beef while preparing the vegetables.
Ready in 30 minutes. Serves 4.

¾ lb.	Top round, flank or blade steak	340 g
1 tbsp.	Cornstarch	15 mL
2 tbsp.	Soy sauce	30 mL
1 tbsp.	Oyster sauce	15 mL
½ tsp.	Granulated sugar	2 mL
	Freshly ground pepper, to taste	
¼ tsp.	Sesame oil	1 mL
1 tbsp.	Vegetable oil	15 mL
2	Garlic cloves, minced	2
1	Medium carrot, sliced thinly on the diagonal	1
1	Medium onion, sliced lengthwise in slivers	1
1	Medium zucchini, sliced in half lengthwise, then on the diagonal	1
8 oz.	Canned sliced water chestnuts, drained	227 mL
1 cup	Frozen kernel corn	250 mL
	Salt, to taste	
	Pepper, to taste	

■ Cut the beef across the grain into very thin slices.
Combine the cornstarch, soy sauce, oyster sauce, sugar,
pepper and sesame oil in a small bowl. Add the beef
and marinate for 15 minutes. ■ Heat the vegetable oil
in a non-stick skillet or wok until hot. Add the garlic
and stir-fry until golden. Add the beef strips with the
marinade, and the carrot and onion. Stir-fry for 3
minutes. Add the zucchini, water chestnuts and corn.
Stir-fry for 2 minutes. Cover and let steam for 3
minutes. ■ Season with salt and pepper.

One serving… Energy 273cal/1144kJ;
Fat 10.5g; Protein 23g; Carbohydrate 24g

Chinese Beef Stir-Fry

Ready in less than 30 minutes. Serve over rice.
Serves 4.

10 oz.	Canned mandarin orange segments, with juice	284 mL
1 tbsp.	Worcestershire sauce	15 mL
¼ cup	Soy sauce	60 mL
1 tsp.	Freshly grated gingerroot	5 mL
1	Garlic clove, minced	1
1 lb.	Round or sirloin tip steak, cut into ¼ x 2 inch (0.6 x 5 cm) strips	454 g
1 tsp.	Vegetable oil	5 mL
1	Medium red or yellow onion, sliced ¼ inch (6 mm) thick	1
2 cups	Fresh snow peas	500 mL
1 cup	Sliced fresh mushrooms	250 mL
1	Green pepper, sliced	1
2 tbsp.	Cornstarch	30 mL
	Reserved mandarin orange segments	

■ Strain the juice from the orange segments and reserve the juice. Set the orange segments aside. ■ Combine the reserved orange juice, Worcestershire sauce, soy sauce, ginger and garlic. Add the beef strips and stir well. Set aside to marinate while cooking the vegetables. ■ Heat the oil in a non-stick skillet or wok until hot. Add the vegetables and stir-fry for 5 minutes. Remove the vegetables to a bowl using a slotted spoon. ■ Remove the beef, reserving the marinade. Stir-fry the beef in the skillet for 3 minutes or until no longer pink. Add the vegetables. ■ Combine the cornstarch with the reserved marinade. Stir into the beef mixture. Heat and stir until thickened. Add the orange segments and stir gently.

One serving… Energy 254cal/1064kJ; Fat 5.6g; Protein 28g; Carbohydrate 23g

Beef with Pea Pods

20 minutes to prepare beef and vegetables and only 10 minutes to cook. Serves 4.

1 lb.	Top round or flank steak	454 g
1 tbsp.	Cornstarch	15 mL
1½ tsp.	Granulated sugar	7 mL
3 tbsp.	Soy sauce	50 mL
3 tbsp.	Oyster sauce	50 mL
⅓ cup	Water	75 mL
1 tbsp.	Vegetable oil	15 mL
2	Small garlic cloves, minced	2
1 tsp.	Freshly grated gingerroot	5 mL
1	Medium onion, sliced lengthwise into wedges	1
2 cups	Fresh pea pods, (or 6 oz.,170 g pkg. frozen, thawed and drained)	500 mL
8 oz.	Canned sliced water chestnuts, drained	227 mL

■ Thinly slice the beef across the grain. Cut into bite size strips. Set aside. ■ Combine the cornstarch, sugar, soy sauce, oyster sauce and water in a small bowl. Set aside. ■ Heat the oil in a non-stick skillet or wok until hot. Add the garlic and ginger. Stir-fry for 30 seconds. ■ Add the onion and stir-fry for 1 minute. ■ Add the pea pods and water chestnuts. Stir-fry for 2 minutes. Remove all the contents of the skillet to a medium bowl. Set aside. ■ Stir-fry the beef strips in 2 batches for 2 to 3 minutes each or until no longer pink. Return all the beef to the skillet. Add the soy sauce mixture. Stir-fry until the mixture is bubbling and thickened. Stir in the vegetables. Cover and simmer for 1 minute to heat through.

One serving… Energy 308cal/1289kJ; Fat 12.2g; Protein 30g; Carbohydrate 19g

Measurement Tables

Throughout this book measurements are given in Conventional and Metric measure. The cup used is the standard 8 fluid ounce. Temperature is given in degrees Fahrenheit and Celsius. Baking pan measurements are in inches and centimeters as well as quarts and liters.

Spoons

Conventional Measure	Metric Measure
¼ teaspoon (tsp.)	1 mL
½ teaspoon (tsp.)	2 mL
1 teaspoon (tsp.)	5 mL
2 teaspoons (tsp.)	10 mL
1 tablespoon (tbsp.)	15 mL

Oven Temperatures

Fahrenheit (°F)	Celsius (°C)
200°	95°
225°	110°
250°	120°
275°	140°
300°	150°
325°	160°
350°	175°
375°	190°
400°	205°
425°	220°
450°	230°
475°	240°
500°	260°

Cups

Conventional Measure	Metric Measure
¼ cup	60 mL
⅓ cup	75 mL
½ cup	125 mL
⅔ cup	150 mL
¾ cup	175 mL
1 cup	250 mL
4 cups	1000 mL (1 L)

Weight Measurements

Ounces (oz.)	Grams (g)
1 oz.	30 g
2 oz.	55 g
3 oz.	85 g
4 oz.	125 g
5 oz.	140 g
6 oz.	170 g
7 oz.	200 g
8 oz.	250 g
16 oz. (1 pound, lb.)	454 g
32 oz. (2 pounds, lbs.)	900 g
2.2 pounds (lbs.)	1000 g (1 kg)

Pans

Conventional Inches	Metric Centimeters (cm)
8 x 8 inch	20 x 20 cm
9 x 9 inch	22 x 22 cm
9 x 13 inch	22 x 33 cm
10 x 15 inch	25 x 38 cm
11 x 17 inch	28 x 43 cm
8 x 2 inch round	20 x 5 cm
9 x 2 inch round	22 x 5 cm
10 x 4½ inch tube	25 x 11 cm
8 x 4 x 3 inch loaf	20 x 10 x 7 cm
9 x 5 x 3 inch loaf	22 x 12 x 7 cm

Casseroles

Conventional Quart (qt.)	Metric Liter (L)
1 qt.	1 L
1½ qt.	1.5 L (1.8 L)
2 qt.	2 L
3 qt.	3 L
4 qt.	4 L (3.8 L)
5 qt.	5 L

Kitchen Equivalents

We sometimes find that our cupboards do not contain the ingredients or cookware called for in a recipe. Or perhaps we haven't had time to do the grocery shopping. What can we substitute? The following is a list of substitutions that might apply when using Beef Today!

Cookware/Bakeware

Casserole Dishes
1½ quart (1.5 L) or 6 x 10 inch (15 x 25 cm) or 8 x 8 inch (20 x 20 cm)
2 quart (2 L) or 8 x 12 inch (20 x 30 cm)
3 quart (3 L) or 9 x 13 inch (22 x 33 cm)

Saucepans
Small or 1½ quart (1.5 L) or 4-6 cups (1-1.5 L)
Medium or 2 quart (2 L) or 8 cups (2 L)
Large or 3-4 quart (3-4 L) or 12-16 cups (3-4 L)
Dutch Oven or 5-6 quart (5-6 L) or 20 cups (5 L)

Skillets
Small or 6-8 inch (15-20 cm)
Medium or 8-10 inch (20-25 cm)
Large or 10-12 inch (25-30 cm)

Ingredients

Beef Broth ◆ 10 oz. (284 mL) can condensed beef broth = 2 tsp. (10 mL) beef bouillon powder plus 1¼ cups (300 mL) boiling water

Flour ◆ 1 tbsp. (15 mL) white flour = 1½ tsp. (7 mL) cornstarch, potato starch, rice starch or arrowstarch

Garlic ◆ 1 medium garlic clove = ¼ tsp. (1 mL) garlic powder

Ginger ◆ 1 tbsp. (15 mL) grated gingerroot = ⅛ tsp. (0.5 mL) ground ginger

Herbs ◆ 1 tbsp. (15 mL) fresh chopped herbs = ½ tsp. (2 mL) dried herbs

Horseradish ◆ 6 oz. (170 g) prepared horseradish = 6 tbsp. (100 mL) dried horseradish

Lemon ◆ 1 tsp. (5 mL) lemon juice (fresh or bottled) = ½ tsp. (2 mL) vinegar

◆ 1 lemon = 2-3 tbsp. (30-50 mL) juice plus 2 tsp. (10 mL) grated peel

Macaroni ◆ 1 cup (250 mL) uncooked macaroni pasta = 2-2¼ cups (500-560 mL) cooked macaroni pasta

◆ 4 cups uncooked macaroni pasta = 1 lb. (454 g) uncooked macaroni pasta

Onion ◆ ¼ cup (60 mL) chopped onion = 1 tbsp. (15 mL) dry onion flakes or 1 tsp. (5 mL) onion powder

Pepper ◆ 1 tsp. (5 mL) freshly grated pepper = ¼ tsp. (1 mL) ground pepper

Sherry ◆ 1 tbsp. (15 mL) sherry = 1 tbsp. (15 mL) cooking sherry or cooking sherry vinegar

White wine ◆ 1 tbsp. (15 mL) white wine = 1 tbsp. (15 mL) white wine vinegar or unsweetened apple juice

Index

187

All in the Family

Company's Coming Cookbooks are available at retail locations everywhere.

For information contact:

COMPANY'S COMING PUBLISHING LIMITED

Box 8037, Station "F"
Edmonton, Alberta
Canada T6H 4N9

Box 17870
San Diego, California
U.S.A. 92177-7870

TEL: (403) 450-6223
FAX: (403) 450-1857